Backpacking Kentucky

Your Guide to the Most Beautiful Trails in the Bluegrass

By
Valerie L. Askren

Backpacking Kentucky
Your Guide to the Most Beautiful Trails in the Bluegrass

Copyright © 2017 by Valerie L. Askren. All rights reserved. No part of this book may be used or reproduced in any manner whatsoever (including electronic means) without written permission, except in case of brief quotations embodied in articles and reviews.

Published by 42nd Parallel, LLC. While not on the trail, we can be reached at HiketheBluegrass@gmail.com.

We also love getting real mail. You can send those old-timey letters to 233 Kingsway Dr., Lexington, KY 40502. If you have any suggestions on improving the book, catch any errors or have any updates, please drop us a line!

ISBN 978-0-692-80396-7

Printed in the United States of America. First edition.

Neither 42nd Parallel LLC, the author, nor anyone else who had anything to do with this book, assumes any responsibility or liability for accidents or injuries suffered by any persons, dogs or hiking poles using this book. This includes anything stupid, silly or accidental you do on or off the trail. You are fully responsible for yourself.

Front Cover
Top: Yahoo Falls, Big South Fork National Recreation Area
Lower: Furnace Arch, Sheltowee Trace, Cave Run Lake
 Bridge over Parched Corn Creek, Red River Gorge
 Vanhook Falls, Cane Creek Wildlife Management Area

Back Cover
Sunset on Half Moon Rock, Red River Gorge—Brian Masylar
See more of Brian's amazing photography at maslyarphoto.com

Acknowledgments
All photos are by the author, with the exception of those generously shared by Ben Askren, Emma Askren, Kevin Bartell, Jade Flores, Tim Flores, Brian Masylar and Kathy Rose. All contributors retain all rights to their photos. The final editing was done by eagle-eye Terese Pierskalla, but all the mistakes are my own. *Thanks everyone!*

The awesome maps were created using QGIS, a free, open-source geographical information system program. Please use and support QGIS. Ben is my personal computer guru who helped me integrate the data from the USGS National Hydrography Dataset and National Elevation Dataset, Open Street Maps, and my own GPS-tracked data.

For Walt, Emma, Rowan and Asa —
may the trails be your path to the Universe.

And for Bear dog —
He never forgets his headlamp, loves my cooking,
and is always ready for the next adventure.

I don't know where I'm going,
but I promise it won't be boring.
~ David Bowie

Contents

Kentucky Trail Locator Map	viii
Trails by Mileage and Configuration	ix
Why on earth would you want to backpack?	1
Ahh...for the Love of Gear!	2

Part I: Overnighters to Multi-Day Trips

Big South Fork National River & Recreation Area 12
   1. Bear Creek Scenic Area 13
   2. Kentucky Trail: Blue Heron to Laurel Crossing Branch 18
   3. Lick Creek and Princess Falls 23
   4. Yahoo Falls Loop 27

Carter Caves State Resort Park 32
   5. Cross Country Trail 32

Cave Run Lake 36
   6. Caney Loop Trail 37
   7. Buckskin Trail 39

Cumberland Gap National Historic Park 45
   8. Ride the Ridge Trail to the Hensley Settlement 45

Land Between the Lakes 50
   9. Canal Loop 52
  10. North/South Trail—North End 55
  11. North/South Trail—South End 60

Mammoth Cave National Park 63
  12. Sal Hollow to Turnhole Bend 66
  13. Bluffs Loop 66
  14. Big Kahuna Loop 66

Pine Mountain State Scenic Trail 68
  15. Birch Knob Section 69
  16. Highland Section 78
  17. Little Shepherd Trail 85

Red River Gorge Geological Area	**88**
18. Auxier Ridge and Double Arch	89
19. Heart of the Gorge	93
Rockcastle River	**102**
20. Rockcastle Narrows West—Bee Rock to Beech Creek	103
21. Rockcastle Narrows East—Vanhook Falls	107
Sheltowee Trace National Recreation Trail	**111**
22. Bark Camp Creek to Dog Slaughter Falls	112
23. Barren Fork	117
24. Mark Branch and Gobbler Arch	121
25. Thru-Hiking the Sheltowee	125

Part 2: Backpacking with Children

Joys and challenges of backpacking with children	**128**
Big South Fork National River & Recreation Area	**131**
A. Blue Heron Loop Trail	131
Land Between the Lakes National Recreation Area	**135**
B. Canal Mini Loop	135
Laurel River Lake	**138**
C. White Oak Boat-In Campground	138
D. Grove Boat-In Campground	138
Mammoth Cave National Park	**142**
E. Homestead	143
F. First Creek Lake	143
G. Three Springs	144
Red River Gorge Geological Area	**145**
H. Chimney Top Creek	145
Sheltowee Trace National Recreation Trail	**148**
I. War Fork Creek & Resurgence Cave	148
About the Author	**151**
Other books of interest	**151**

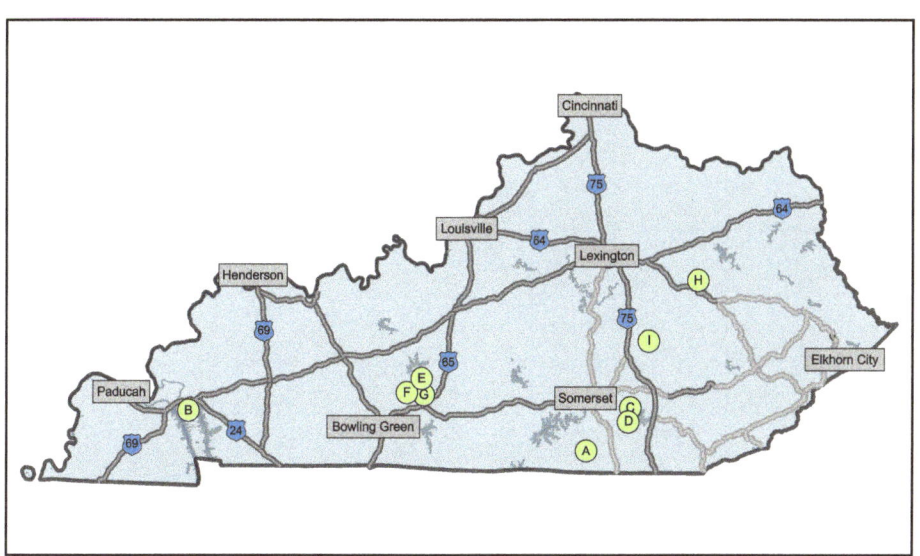

Kid-Friendly Trails

Trails	Mileage	Configuration
A. Blue Heron Loop Trail	6.2	*Loop*
B. Canal Mini Loop	3.7	*Balloon loop*
C. White Oak Campground	2 - 3	*Out-and-back (round trip)*
D. Grove Campground	1.5	*Out-and-back (round trip)*
E. Homestead	4.4	*Out-and-back (round trip)*
F. First Creek Lake	2.2	*Out-and-back (round trip)*
G. Three Springs	1.6	*Out-and-back (round trip)*
H. Chimney Top Creek	2 - 4.6	*Out-and-back (round trip)*
I. War Fork Creek	3 - 5	*Out-and-back (round trip)*

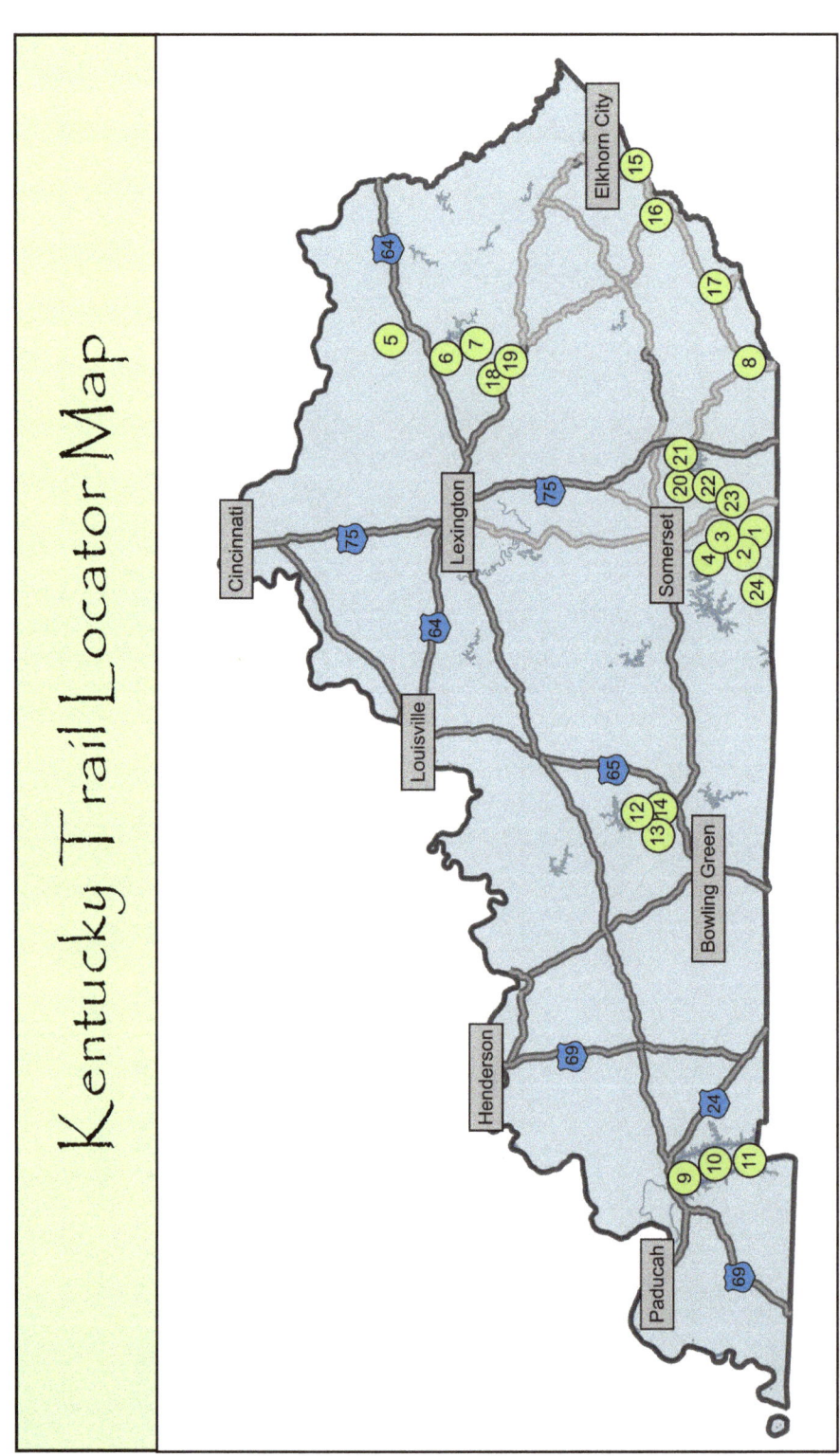

Trails by Mileage and Configuration

Trails	Mileage	Configuration
Big South Fork		
1. Bear Creek Scenic Area	19.8	*Triple loop trail*
2. Kentucky Trail	10.2 - 14.7	*Out-and-back or balloon loop*
3. Lick Creek and Princess Falls	11.7 - 20.9	*Out-and-back or balloon loop*
4. Yahoo Falls Loop	9.2	*Loop*
Carter Caves State Resort Park		
5. Cross Country Trail	8.0	*Loop*
Cave Run Lake		
6. Caney Loop Trail	8.5	*Loop*
7. Buckskin Trail	13.7 - 19.4	*Variety of configurations*
Cumberland Gap National Historic Park		
8. Ridge Trail to Hensley	20+	*One-way (can easily shorten)*
Land Between the Lakes		
9. Canal Loop	11.0	*Loop*
10. North/South Trail—North End	31.0	*One-way (can easily shorten)*
11. North/South Trail—South End	27.0	*One-way (can easily shorten)*
Mammoth Cave National Park		
12. Sal Hollow to Turnhole Bend	10.0	*Out-and-back*
13. Bluffs Loop	12.9	*Loop*
14. Big Kahuna Loop	31.4	*Double loops*
Pine Mountain State Scenic Trail		
15. Birch Knob Section	29.6	*One-way*
16. Highland Section	16 - 18.2	*One-way*
17. Little Shepherd Trail	14 - 38	*One-way (can shorten)*
Red River Gorge Geological Area		
18. Auxier Ridge and Double Arch	8.9	*Balloon loop*
19. Heart of the Gorge	29.7 - 32.1	*Loop and double-back*
Rockcastle River		
20. Bee Rock to Beech Creek	7.0	*Loop (mostly)*
21. Vanhook Falls	11.6	*Balloon loop*
Sheltowee Trace National Trail		
22. Bark Camp to Dog Slaughter	10.9	*One-way*
23. Barren Fork	9.0	*One-way*
24. Mark Branch and Gobbler Arch	8.1	*Balloon loop*
25. Thru-Hiking the Sheltowee	322.5	*One-way (can easily shorten)*

Why on earth would you want to backpack?

For many years, backpacking has taken a backseat to what some would argue are more exciting outdoor sports. Personally, a long time ago I happily ditched my slow-moving REI Valhalla pack for a rock-hoppin' mountain bike and a playful whitewater kayak. I guess for me, it was the need for speed and that rush of adrenaline that made me feel alive.

But in the last few years I have noticed a huge resurgence in interest by people wanting to strap an ungodly amount of weight onto their backs, only to set up their tent in the pouring rain, sit on a termite-infested log, and devour an overpriced pouch of rehydrated organic quinoa with kale flakes. Who brought the bourbon?

Yet somehow, backpackers are a hardy bunch who shirk pop culture and now we're seeing not only second, but also third-generation backpackers taking to the trails. Honestly, I think it has to do with people wanting to live simply. In this world of overconsumption, more and more people are realizing that all you really need in life is in your heart and on your back.

Backpacking allows you to see things that are out-of-reach during a typical day hike. There is more opportunity to find solitude; to distinguish between a barred owl and a screech owl; to watch the sun rise or the sun set; to stretch your aching legs in front of a warm fire; or stand beneath a waterfall or on top of the world. At its core, backpacking is essentially the path for hikers who never want to leave the trail. Plus, backpacking is relatively cheap. It's pretty easy to throw a trip together. And you can make it as painless or as challenging as you want.

Why *Backpacking Kentucky*? Because there's no book out there! Further, try and Google the phrase. Nada. Go to our state's Adventure Tourism web site. Ninguno. Backpacking is not even listed! Yet every year hardy souls trek here, looking to be submerged in the rugged beauty of Kentucky. But unfortunately, everyone seems to keep going to the same places and hiking the same trails. Believe it or not, there *are* trails outside of the Red River Gorge.

Hence you are holding *Backpacking Kentucky*, your personal guide to the best backcountry trails in the state. Written for both beginner and experienced backpackers, we want to get you off the beaten path and into the backwoods of the Bluegrass. Endowed with a proliferation of natural bridges and sandstone arches, rhododendron thickets, towering hemlocks, spring-fed creeks, gorgeous wildflowers, and hardwood forests, Kentucky has an impressive array of overnight options for the backcountry adventurer.

Hikes are divided into two categories—Part 1 focuses on simple overnight trips and multi-day forays into the wilderness. Part 2 highlights shorter trails to introduce the next generation of hikers to the joys of backpacking. Each entry includes explicit directions to the trailhead (TH); a detailed map with suggested campsites; comprehensive trail and route descriptions; plus interesting tidbits about the ecology and culture of the area.

So enjoy the trails and may you find your own outdoor nirvana.

Ahh...for the Love of Gear!

The old school of thought would have you believe that you'd be a fool to take on nature without arming yourself with every conceivable measure of safety and comfort under the sun. But that isn't what being in nature is all about. Rather, it's about feeling free, unbounded, shedding the distractions and barriers of our civilization—not bringing them with us.

Ryel Kestenbaum, The Ultralight Backpacker

You have to love that quote. Yet it seems to be the antithesis of this section. But all sports require gear and with backpacking your comfort and your livelihood depend on it. And with outdoor gear, you basically get what you pay for. But you don't need to buy everything new and you don't have to buy everything at once. Start with the most important items and add to your collection as you can afford to or even look for good used equipment. Try to add one new piece of top-notch equipment each year, with an eye on quality and weight.

What follows is a brief overview of the gear most people take backpacking. There's already tons of info on the Internet, so we're going to keep it basic here. If you know all this, just skip on to the next section.

Footwear

On the trail, sturdy, good-fitting boots are your best friend. Go to an outfitter you trust, tell them what you want to do, and then try on lots of pairs until you get this right. You want boots that are waterproof, preferably ankle-high with good arch support, and feel good right out of the box. Pay special attention to the toe box. Don't be misled into thinking that only after you have "broken" them in, they will feel good to your feet. They should feel good from day one, and even better every day after that.

While some people prefer full-leather uppers, other hikers choose boots comprised of man-made materials to reduce weight and cost. Leather boots can be quite heavy and hot in the summer, but their durability is unequaled. Regardless, you want a quality boot that fits well, so you can avoid succumbing to foot fatigue. I've seen people backpacking in sneakers and Chacos, but I don't recommend it. If your feet aren't feeling good, you're going nowhere fast.

Waterproof boots typically translates to the boot being made with a Gore-Tex or similar liner. Even if it's not raining, multiple creek-crossings and deep puddles can make wet feet miserable. And be sure to thoroughly dry out your boots (and other gear) before putting things away after a trip.

While you're checking out footwear, review your sock inventory. Thickness depends on personal preference and time of year, but don't be misled thinking that the thicker the socks, the less likely you are to get blisters. You want something that wicks so the moisture generated by hiking doesn't get your feet warm and damp. That means no cotton or cotton blends. Many backpackers swear by merino wool and prefer brand names such as Icebreaker, SmartWool, or even REI. You may need to experiment with a few different choices until you find what is right for you and your feet.

Backpacks

Yes, while you're at the outfitter, be sure to check out their packs. Again, explain what type of backpacking you'll be doing and listen closely to their recommendations. The store can fill packs with various weights and strap the pack on you so you can test them out.

Pack size has two dimensions: relative to your body and relative to the length of trip you typically want to do. As for selecting a pack relative to your body size, packs typically come in small, medium or large. Leg length is not particularly important here—it's torso length that matters. Most of the better packs come with an adjustable torso length. Several manufacturers also offer gender-specific packs, which can be particularly important to get the proper hip and shoulder fit. Finally, some hip belts can be warm-molded in the store for a customized personal fit.

Pack size itself varies only slightly with trip length. Regardless of how many days you'll be out, you still need the basics including a tent, sleeping bag, cookware and so forth. The biggest variable is how much food you will need and how many clothes you'll pack (which is based in large part on weather conditions). Generally speaking, you'll want to consider 30- to 50-liter packs for overnight or weekend jaunts, and 50- to 80-liter packs for multi-day trips. If you can manage, a 50-liter pack (around 3,000 cubic inches) is a good all around pack size that forces you to economize on what you bring on the trail. But make sure all your gear will fit in before you leave the store.

Other considerations include pockets to easily stash water bottles versus a water bladder; if the pack has a built-in rain cover or a removable daypack; a mesh back panel (keeps you cool on warm days); and a separate sleeping bag compartment. Most packs these days are top-loading, internal frames, but other choices are available.

Look very carefully at the weight of the pack. Your unloaded pack should weigh less than 5 pounds and there are several excellent options in the 2.5- to 4.5-pound range. While this may not seem like a lot of weight difference, on the trail it sure does! So do a little Internet research, read the reviews, and talk with your outfitter.

Finally, talk to your outfitter or do some more research on the proper way to load your pack. Proper weight distribution is critical to avoid shoulder and back fatigue.

I just can't get this dog to mush.

Backpacking Kentucky

Backpacking Tents

Tent choices are endless and research can be a huge time sink. Three-season or four-season tent? Freestanding or needs staking? One-person or two or three? Or maybe just a hammock or bivy sack is all you need. But if you choose one of the latter options, be sure to give it a good overnight test to make sure you're compatible.

Most importantly, you need a quality tent that you can trust, complete with sealed seams and a ground cloth. To test if it's waterproof, take it outside and repeatedly squirt it with a hose. You do NOT want a leaking tent, which translates into wet gear and a miserable trip. And always be sure your footprint or ground cloth does not extend beyond the outer edge of the tent itself. Otherwise, water can hit the ground cloth and roll right under your tent, creating puddles between the bottom of your tent and the footprint.

One of the mysteries of tent buying is size selection. A solo tent has room for you, but not much gear. A 2-man tent has room for you and your gear. A 3-man tent holds two people, but not much gear. So consider vestibule size if you need to keep your gear outside your tent. And don't assume that sharing a tent with your hiking partner will necessarily save you weight—some 2- and 3-man tents weigh more than twice what two solo tents weigh. But there are plenty of other excellent reasons to share a tent while out on the trail.

Your tent should be lightweight, which means a solo tent should weigh in at three pounds or less for everything (tent, fly, poles, stakes, footprint, and stuff sack). Similarly, a 2-person tent should weigh less than five pounds and 3- or 4-person tents should weigh less than eight pounds. But usually there is an ounces to dollar spent trade-off in tent selection.

Getting into the swing of things. (B. Askren)

Backpacking Kentucky

Hammocks

Hammocks are the current cool thing. They show up in the woods. In city parks. On front porches. Back yards. Even across creeks. Importantly, hammock design has improved with super-easy strap and carabiner systems, bug nets, and waterproof tarps. But don't go this route if your only motivation is to save on weight. A single-nest Eno system weighs in at 2 pounds 13 ounces, about the same as a good quality solo tent.

But hammocks can also bring freedom to the backpacking junkie who is looking to pitch sleeping space on a 45-degree incline or over large rocks and logs. Although you will probably still want a sleeping pad and bag, you can avoid the hard ground and that tree root in the small of your back by overnighting in a hammock.

Yet not everyone can sleep in a hammock and not all couples will love each other as much after a restless night in a double-nest sling. If possible, try and borrow a good hammock system for a trial run before you make that purchase.

Sleeping Bags

Sleeping well on the trail is paramount to having a good time. The traditional trade-off was between synthetics (bulkier, yet cheaper) and down (lighter, compacts smaller, but more expensive). But some of the new bags utilize pre-treated down to keep the feathers from getting damp, thus picking up weight and losing their ability to keep you warm. Buy what you can afford and choose a bag weight for the weather conditions you will most likely encounter. Then for Christmas, ask for other sleeping bags to add to your stable of options so you can backpack year-round.

You should also seriously consider a good sleeping pad. Your basic choice will be between an air pad (or mattress) and a foam pad. As always, the sweet spot lies in the nexus of weight, comfort, and price. For the rocky conditions of Kentucky, a nice lightweight air mattress on top of a mini-cell foam pad can be ideal.

Potable Water

Fortunately Kentucky has an abundance of water sources and typically you don't have to lug all of your water. Also keep in mind that a gallon of water weighs about 8.3 pounds, so you'll only want to carry enough water to safely get you to the next reliable water source. And never drink from an untreated water source, regardless of how clear it looks.

Options for treating water are many, each with their own advantages and drawbacks. Popular options are filters (including gravity-fed, pumps, LifeStraw, and squeeze filtering systems) and SteriPENs. Some hikers still use water purification tablets and iodine, which are good back-ups in case your primary system fails. Regardless of which system you choose, make absolutely sure you know how to properly use it before you get on the trail.

Gravity-fed filters are great for groups.

5

Backpacking Kentucky

Stoves, Fuel and Cookware

There are a multitude of choices here. Again, do your research, read the reviews, and talk to your outfitter. You want something simple, reliable, and lightweight. Be sure to test your stove out several times before hitting the trail. Fuel choice is stove-dependent—just don't forget to bring it. Cookware should also be simple and lightweight. One small to medium-sized pan with lid, possibly a mug, and a spoon or Spork is all that you really need.

Food

There are two dimensions to food – what to eat and how to store it. Let's tackle the last one first. Due to bear and critter activity in Kentucky, food storage restrictions are in place for most areas (such as the Red River Gorge) and highly suggested in other areas.

Your basic options are to either "hang" your food and trash, or use a bear-resistant container. Hanging your food items (including other "smell-ables" such as toothpaste, bug repellent or anything else that might smell "good") requires a length of line, plus a bag to hold everything (typically made out of a waterproof material or Kevlar). The bag should be hung at least ten feet off the ground and four feet away from any tree or post used for suspension. The Pacific Coast Trail method uses 40 feet of line, a carabiner, bag, and a small stick to effectively hang food.

No bear could escape these canisters.

Another option is to carry a bear-resistant food container, including Bear Vaults or canisters that do not require hanging, but are heavier to carry as compared with some lines and carabiners. Arguments pro and con can be made for both approaches and depend more on personal preference. If you choose a bear-resistant canister, be sure it will fit into your pack.

As for eating, food preferences are all over the board. Some backpackers drink tea for breakfast, eat an energy bar for lunch, and feast on ramen noodles for dinner. Others prefer buying packaged dehydrated meals, which can be easy, but also pricey, high in fat and sodium content, and sometimes less than tasty.

But you might want to check out the newer freeze-dried meals, made by companies such as Mountain House. Ignoring the eco-NOT-friendly packaging, they are much improved over the previous dehydrated versions. You can also buy lots of different freeze-dried foods on-line, including meats (chicken to crumbled sausage), veggies (kale flakes to cauliflower), and fruit (organic mangoes to pomegranate powder). North Bay Trading Company even has tofu and a humongous list of Certified Kosher air- and freeze-dried foods. Now, if they could just freeze-dry ice cold beer….

Many backpacking purists will dehydrate their own meals, particularly dinners. Scope out ideas on the Internet and don't be afraid to try different combinations. If you're hungry enough, you'll eat anything. But the price of a new dehydrator will easily pay for itself in no time.

Backpacking Kentucky

If you are going to rehydrate food for dinner, consider starting the process while you're setting up camp. Mix the morsels and water in the cook pot, pre-heat if desired, set-aside in a safe place with a heavy rock on top, and let the hydrogen and oxygen molecules work their magic. Once your tent is up and bed made, dinner is close at hand.

Clothing

Backpacking is not a time for a fashion, and not even for clean clothes. Functionality is what it's all about. Don't be afraid to wear the same thing on the trail day after day. Extra clothing can really weigh your pack down. There's no sense saving every ounce on gear, only to throw in two extra t-shirts and a third pair of long pants.

Always think in layers. While on the trail it's easy to overheat, but around camp during the evening or early morning, a chill can set in. Again—try to avoid cotton and reach for those wicking fabrics that can keep you warm when they get damp and are quick to dry if they get wet. Tops with zip necks are always great for venting.

For the most part, rain gear is a must. Gore-Tex is always nice, but it's a pricey option, too. Look for sealed seams and hip-length jackets with an adjustable hood. Rain pants are always great to throw on over your shorts or long pants for an extra layer of warmth, instead of simply bringing more clothes. A pair of thin gloves, neck gaiter, and a lightweight fleece or wool hat can also work wonders in cooler months.

Personal Items

Other good items to have on the trail include:
- Headlamp
- Waterproof matches and/or lighter
- First-aid kit, including blister relief
- Compass
- Knife
- Small trowel for burying human waste
- Trekking poles – good for knees and shoulders
- Insect repellent

And the list goes on! If we were all boy scouts, we would be much better prepared. But we might not be able to lift our packs.

Save the Dutch ovens for base camp.

Sharing Gear

There are two schools of thought here. One is that every person should be totally self-contained with a complete set of gear. The second paradigm is that certain items can be shared within a group, as long as there are back-ups. Good examples include stoves, cookware and water filters. Not everyone in your group might need to have a stove. But there should be two stoves amongst the members of the group in case of equipment failure. Just be sure before you set out that everyone has brought what is expected in terms of group gear. Similar arguments can be made for sharing meals, particularly dinners.

Human Waste Disposal

Definitely not a fun topic, but one that needs discussing. The recommended methods for disposing of human feces are either digging a cathole and burying the waste, or using a wag bag.

To dig a cathole, find a private spot at least 200 feet from any trail, water source, campsite or other frequently used place. Dig the hole 6 to 8 inches deep, and 4 to 6 inches wide. After making your deposit, re-cover with the excavated soil and other natural materials (such as a rock or small log). All toilet paper should be packed out; alternately, natural materials such as leaves can be used and buried with the waste.

There are other waste disposal products out there, such as a WAG bag kit, which includes a strong waste-collecting bag, a petite amount of toilet paper, a small amount of powdered gelling compound, and a single hand sanitizer wipe packet. After using, all this gets dropped into a ziplock-style bag for you to carry out. (Just don't sling it into the woods somewhere!)

Leave No Trace

Last, let's end on a note about Leave No Trace Principles. Widely adopted and respected around the world, leave no trace principles basically assure that we leave nature just as we found it. As our population grows and our natural areas shrink, it is everyone's responsibility to minimize the adverse impact we have on our earth. The guidelines outlined below have been simplified for this book.

- Prepare and plan ahead
- Bring maps, proper gear, food, and water
- Stay on trails
- Walk single file in the middle of the trail (unless it is wide such as an old logging road) and avoid erosive practices
- Leave rocks, plants, animals, and other artifacts
- Help keep wildlife wild
- Respect wildlife, particularly during breeding, nesting, and birthing seasons
- Respect private property
- Human waste—If necessary, dig a 6-8" cat hole at least 200' from water, trails, and campsites. Pack out all toilet paper.
- Hike in small groups, use quiet tones, leave music systems at home
- If you packed it in, then pack it out!

Basically this is an updated list combining "Do unto others" with "take only pictures, leave only footprints" philosophies. For more information, go to the Leave No Trace website at Lnt.org.

Backpacking Kentucky

T. Flores

As soon as i saw you,
i knew an adventure was going to happen.
~ Winnie the Pooh

Part I: Overnighters to Multi-Day Trips

In every walk with nature, one receives far more than he seeks.
~ John Muir

Big South Fork National River & Recreation Area

The Big South Fork National River and Recreation Area (BSF) straddles the Kentucky/Tennessee border and protects the Big South Fork of the Cumberland River and many of its tributaries. The 76-mile river is one of the most prominent features in the park and the erosive power of the water created much of the exquisite scenery found here. In addition, the Big South Fork River is a world-class whitewater destination, attracting kayakers and canoeists from all over the United States.

The geology of the region has also created one of the highest concentrations of natural arches in the United States, second only to Utah. The BSF is graced with majestic sandstone bluffs, intimate gorges, and innumerable rockhouses or shelters. Not surprisingly, the BSF attracts a large number of rock climbers to its challenging environs.

While pines, mountain laurel, and blueberry bushes dominate the ridgetops, at lower elevations the creeks are lined with hemlock, fern, and moss-shrouded boulders. The ecosystem of the BSF is very similar to that found in the Red River Gorge. But the Gorge, at 29,000 acres, carries a much higher density of visitors as compared with the Big South Fork, which covers 125,000 acres. So solitude at the BSF is much easier to find and much easier to keep.

In summary, the Big South Fork is a popular destination for good reason. It's simply a spectacularly beautiful area. Hikers, backpackers, equestrian riders, hunters, paddlers, and fishermen all love the BSF. And to accommodate the various needs of these diverse groups, the park service has developed trails of all kinds, including those open to ATVers. As a consequence, careful trail selection is paramount to ensure a good time.

Regulations: Overnight camping in the Big South Fork requires a permit, but prices are more than reasonable. For example, for a group of 1-6 people, up to 14 days, a backcountry permit will set you back 5 bucks. Yes, that's $5 total. You can purchase the permit at the Bandy Creek Visitor Center, the Blue Heron Interpretive Center, some private vendors, and on-line. Keep your permit with you at all times.

There are no developed backcountry sites. To minimize impact, try to use an existing campsite rather than creating a new one. Camping is not permitted within 200 feet of any developed area or 25 feet from any trail, cave, grave site, historic structure, road, or rockshelter. Always practice Leave No Trace Principles.

Remember to secure your food and trash from predators. All food must be properly stored in a bear vault (canister) or hung with approved hanging techniques. At night, it's a good idea to hang your backpack, too. Pets are permitted, but must be kept on leash not to exceed 6-feet in length. Campfires are also permitted with the usual precautions.

For more information on camping at the BSF, call (423) 286–7275 or go to tinyurl.com/BSFcamping.

Big South Fork National River & Recreation Area:
1. Bear Creek Scenic Area

A triple-loop, trifecta of a backpacking trip, combining the Lee Hollow, Bear Creek and Cotton Patch loop trails.

Trail Length: 19.8 miles
Suggested Time: 3 days / 2 nights
Maps: National Geographic Trails Illustrated: Big South Fork
OutrageGIS.com: Sheltowee Trace—South

Overview: The Bear Creek Scenic Area is, well, incredibly scenic. But few people go here and even fewer hike the trails or backpack overnight. But let's get this out up front—these are horse trails that are also open to hikers. And most hikers avoid horse trails like the plague due to the deplorable conditions of many trails open to equestrian riders.

But all in all, these trails are in great shape. Yes, there are a few muddy quagmires and deeply eroded sections, particularly the closer you get to the horse camp. But for the most part, these trails are a joy to hike along. The wide trail, high canopy, and deep shade result in fewer insects, spider webs, and poison ivy interfering with your hike. It's also nice not to have to watch your footing every second and be able to gaze at the beautiful scenery around you as you hike. And best of all, except during holidays and pretty spring and fall weekends, chances are you won't see another soul out on the trail. Highlights include multiple spring-fed creek drainages, the Big South Fork River, and the impressive Split Bow Arch.

Directions: South of Whitley City, KY turn west on KY 92. Drive 1.3 miles. Turn left on KY 1651, at the sign for Blue Heron and the Bear Creek Scenic Area. Drive 1.0 mile. Take a sharp right-hand turn on KY 742. Drive 3.1 miles. Turn left on an unmarked road, also signed for the Bear Creek Scenic Area. Drive 2.0 miles. Stay straight at the next intersection. Continue on the gravel road for another 0.4 miles. Turn right at the sign for the Bear Creek Horse Camp. In 0.7 miles the road ends at the campground. Trailhead parking is in the lot on your right.

Staging: Camping is available at Bear Creek Horse Camp, located at the trailhead. The campground has 22 sites, all with electric, and a bathhouse with hot showers. Rates are $28 per night. The campground is usually empty during the week and only gets busy during holiday weekends. No, you don't need to bring a horse to camp here. But be forewarned, the horse crowd is a fun-loving group and may get rowdy.

Route Description: The Bear Creek Scenic Area is basically comprised of three loops—the Lee Hollow, Bear Creek, and Cotton Patch Loop Trails. Hikers can easily do one or all three loops, but the proposed route combines all three. Similarly, you can hike the loops in any direction and in any order. However, campsites are somewhat limited if you're looking for that magical nexus of flat space, water, and scenic views.

Backpacking Kentucky

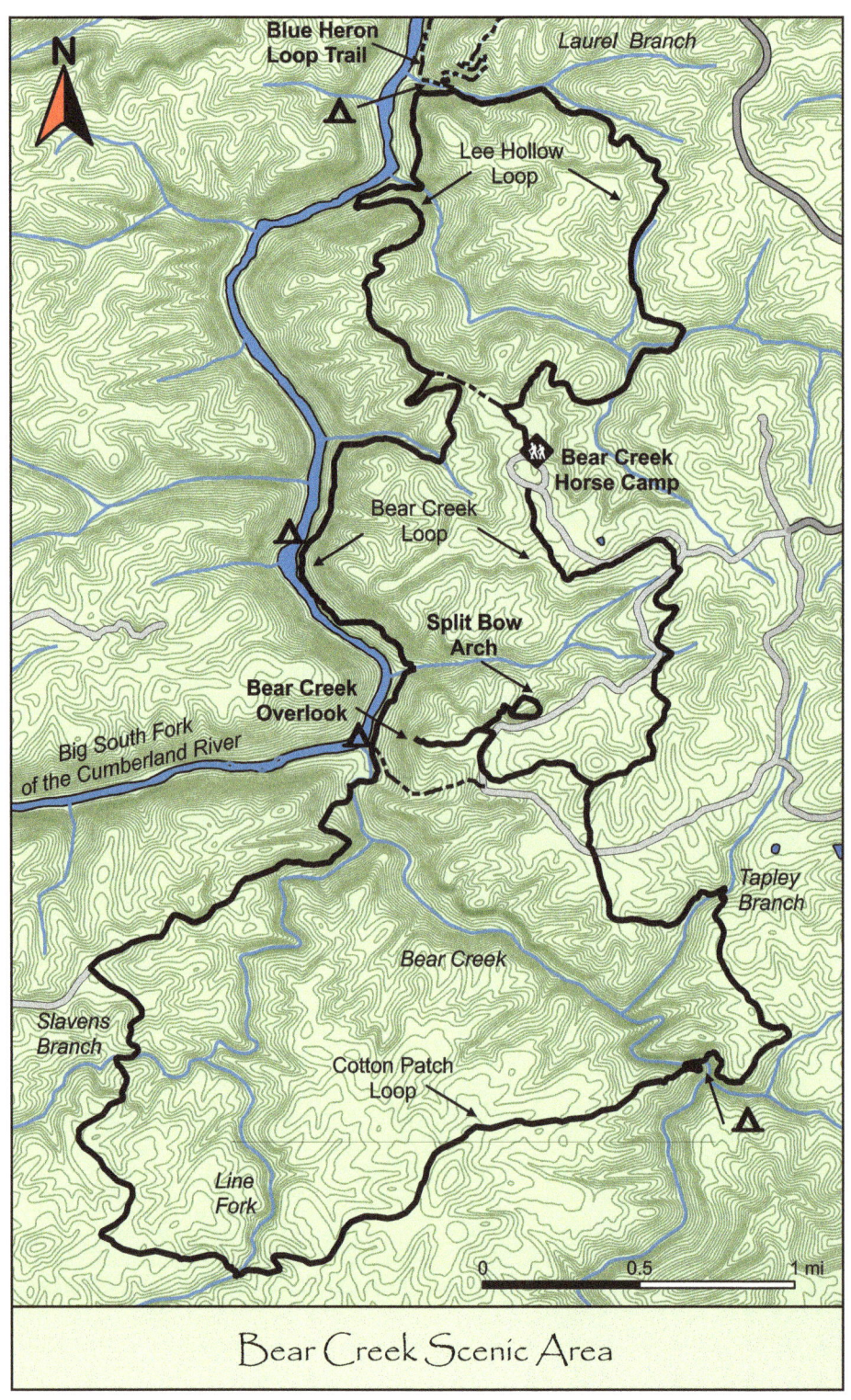

The route described below is as follows:
   Connector trail from Horse Camp to Lee Hollow Loop—0.4 miles
   Lee Hollow Loop Trail (counterclockwise)—4.5 miles
   Bear Creek Loop Trail (west side)—2.5 miles
   Cotton Patch Loop Trail (counterclockwise)—8 miles
   Spur to Overlook and Arch— 2.5 miles
   Return along Bear Creek Loop Trail (east side)—1.9 miles

From the parking lot at Bear Creek Horse Camp, follow the Perimeter Trail, which leaves from the far end of the lot and encircles the campground. This will take you to the short 0.2-mile connector trail, which is also accessible between campsites 8 and 9. At the end of the connector trail, turn right (east) and follow the Lee Hollow Loop Trail. The wide path is perfect for walking next to your best hiking buddy, which may be your canine companion. After passing several nice rockhouses, the trail joins a small creek. Head upstream just a ways, until you see the trail splitting off to your left.

Just past an old foundation (also on your left), the trail hits Laurel Branch, a wonderful spring-fed creek that murmurs quietly as it makes it's way through the deeply shaded canopy of stately hemlocks. If you crossed the creek and followed that trail, it would take you to the Blue Heron Mining Camp. But you want to bear left, to stay on the Lee Hollow Loop Trail. Just on the other side of that gorgeous, two-story, house-sized boulder (shrouded in deep green moss, Mother Nature's original shag carpet) is a small, older campsite within wonderful earshot of the small waterfall that tumbles nearby. Beyond this point, the trail climbs for about 1.25 miles, which gives you an inkling of things to come.

After hiking for about 4.5 miles on the Lee Hollow Loop Trail, bear right (south) on the Bear Creek Loop Trail (continuing straight would take you back to the horse camp). From here the trail makes a steep descent down to the river. Once you reach the Big South Fork of the Cumberland River, glimpses of the water are intermittent, particularly once the trees leaf out. As the trail parallels the river, you'll see a small, sandy campsite with good water access on your right. Hiking further along the Bear Creek Loop, you'll pass a newer river gauging station (in a brown, wood-sided building) and then an older gauging station (in a chimney-tower of sorts). Changes in water levels are not only important for fishermen and paddlers, but for monitoring flood levels.

Winding path on Bear Creek Loop.

Backpacking Kentucky

Just past the old gauging station, Bear Creek Loop bears left up the hill toward the Overlook. You'll want to stay straight here, to follow the Cotton Patch Loop Trail. There is another sandy beach campsite just past this intersection, off a small trail on your right. The housekeeping skills of previous campers could be a little better, but the views and water access are great.

Staying on the Cotton Patch Loop, you will soon ford Bear Creek. Having a good pair of water shoes is always helpful in a situation like this one. Recent rains may cause tremendous variation in water levels, but typically there is a small rocky shoal just downstream of the trail crossing proper, which may be a little easier to ford. The trail leading out of the creek drainage takes you up, and up, and up. While the ascent may be a bit tiresome, keep reminding yourself you're not inside trying to find that one small error in all those lines of code or draining grease from a basket of fries. You have to love the quiet here.

Bear, patiently waiting in the green depths of Tapley Branch.

Big South Fork

In a little over a mile, the trail passes through a gate and follows a gravel road. In 0.35 miles, bear left to stay on the Cotton Patch Loop. All the trails here are very well marked, so you should not have any trouble. (However, the mileage indicators are a little suspect.) Once you reach Line Fork, you are basically standing on the Kentucky/Tennessee state border. In another 0.4 miles, you'll take another left to stay on Cotton Patch Loop—again, well marked. There are several flat camping spots up on this ridge, but no water is available.

In less than 2 miles you'll reach Bear Creek again, this time in the upper drainage. This is a beautiful spot. You can easily imagine eons ago the creek, screaming at high water levels, eroding the base of the majestic sandstone cliffs. Here the trail crosses the creek once more (again, look for the rocky shoal downstream for easier crossing). On the other side of the creek there is a nice campsite lying deep within the shade of more towering hemlocks, with a rockhouse for a nice visual backdrop. Consider hanging your hammock here, listening to the sounds of the creek, and perhaps washing off the grime of the day.

From the second Bear Creek crossing, you have 1.9 miles of hiking, a gravel road crossing, and another 0.3 miles before reaching the intersection of the Bear Creek and Cotton Patch loop trails. Take a left here to hike to the Bear Creek Overlook and Split Bow Arch Trail. Walk for 0.4 miles, turn right on the gravel road, and then hike another 0.2 miles. You'll see the signs for both trails on your left. At one time, the Bear Creek Overlook was considered one of the best views of the Big South Fork River. But trees now block much of this view, rendering it a bit anti-climatic.

But the lollipop loop trail to Split Bow Arch is well worth your time. Follow the trail for 0.3 miles, down multiple steps painstakingly cut into the rock. At the fork, bear left to follow the short 0.4-mile loop trail clockwise. The arch is amazing and rarely visited. Be sure to savor the moment.

After visiting Split Bow Arch, retrace your steps back to where Bear Creek and Cotton Patch loop trails joined. Stay straight to follow the Bear Creek Loop Trail for 1.9 miles back to the horse camp. Yes, there are a few muddy quagmires along the way, but all together Bear Creek Scenic Area has some great trails.

Climbing through Split Bow Arch.

Big South Fork National River & Recreation Area: 2. Kentucky Trail: Blue Heron to Laurel Crossing Branch

Lots of eye candy on this hike.

Trail Length: 10.2 miles (to Laurel Branch and back); 14.7 miles (includes river loop)
Suggested Time: 2 days / 1 night; 3 days / 2 nights
Maps: OutrageGIS.com: Sheltowee Trace—South
National Geographic Trails Illustrated: Big South Fork
National Park Service trail brochure: tinyurl.com/glofdph (partial map)

Overview: The backpacking trail starts from the Blue Heron Mining Camp, an outdoor museum run by the National Park Service. Although it's an out-and-back hike, unless you have eyes in the back of your head, it's just as pretty hiking one way as it is hiking the other direction. Highlights include the tipple bridge, Catawba and Dick Gap Overlooks, and both Dick Gap and Big Spring Falls. The scenery is classic Big South Fork—towering hemlocks, crystal-clear streams, and great rockhouses.

You could do this hike in less time, but there is so much to enjoy, why hurry? You could easily spend 2-3 hours at the Blue Heron outdoor museum, before hiking into the Catawba Overlook area or Laurel Crossing. And be sure to do all the side trails—they are what make this trip worthwhile.

Honestly, the section from Laurel Crossing to the river is nice, but not spectacular. But the two cemeteries found along the way are interesting—Arizona King and Emily Watson, where are you today? And camping down on the river is always fun. Maybe next time you could do a float trip….

Directions: From Whitley City, KY follow US 27 south. Turn right (west) on KY 92 and drive for 1.3 miles. Turn left (south) on KY 1651. Drive for 0.5 miles. Turn right (west) on KY 741 and follow for 0.7 miles. Take another right on KY 742 until you reach the Big South Fork National River and Recreation Area. Stay on KY 742 until it dead-ends at the mining camp. You can park in any of the lots and safely leave a vehicle overnight.

Staging: If you want to ease into this overnighter, you can stay at the Blue Heron Campground. There also is free camping right near the trailhead on the river, just upstream of the mining camp. See the Blue Heron Loop Trail description in the kid's backpacking section for more information.

Route Description: Begin your adventure by crossing the tipple bridge from the mining camp parking lot. Built in the 1930s, the bridge carried tram cars along narrow gauge rail lines, bringing coal from mines located across the river. The converted pedestrian bridge offers excellent views up and down the river and access to the trailhead on the other side. Blue Heron is also a popular put-in for paddlers going downstream to Yamacraw Bridge or Alum Ford.

Big South Fork

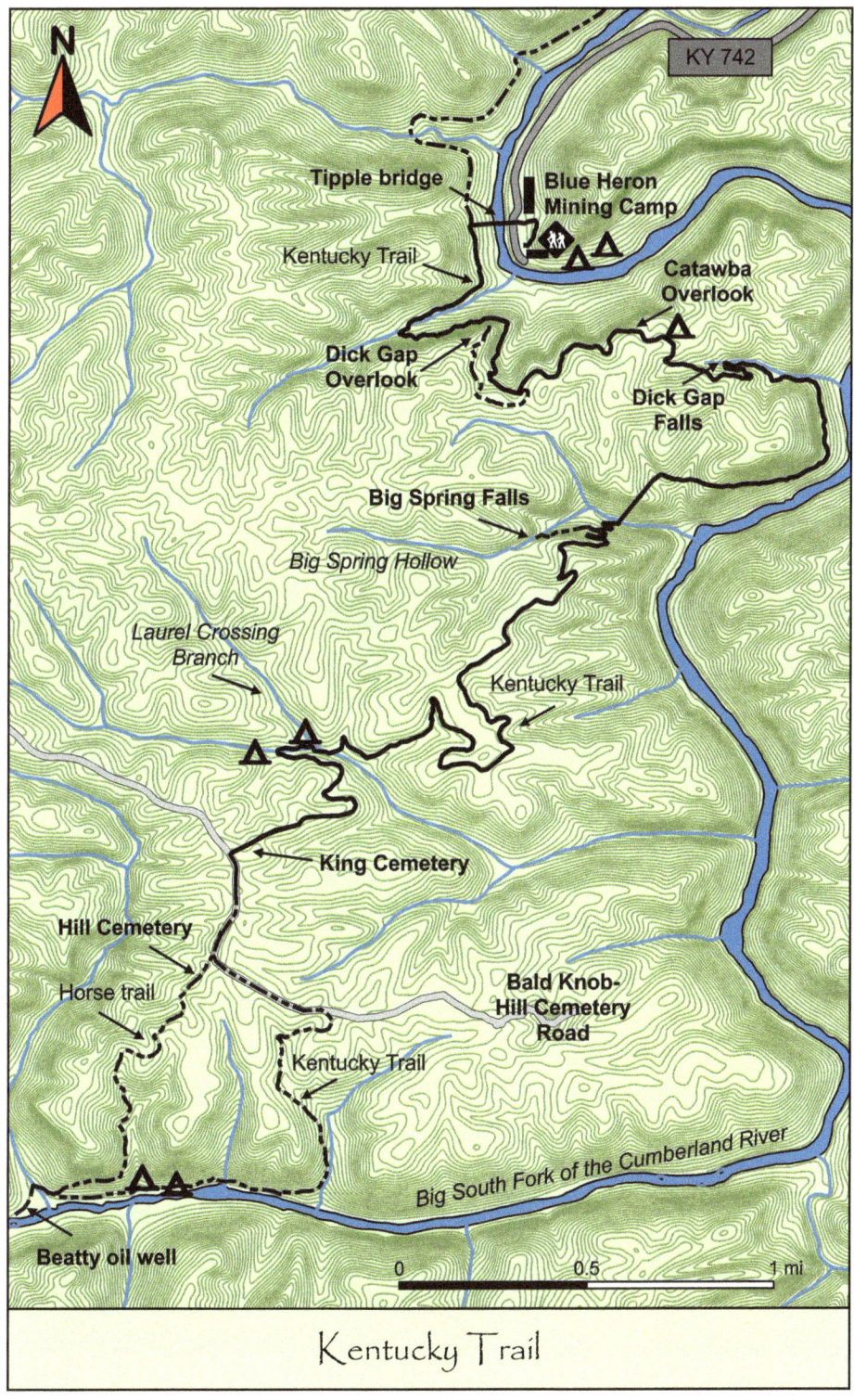

Kentucky Trail

Tipple bridge at Blue Heron Mining Camp.

Once across the bridge, turn left (south) toward the Ledbetter Trailhead, Oil Well Branch, and Catawba Overlook. The first section of the trail follows an old rail bed, sans rails, with occasional evidence of the history made here. An old, abandoned tram car and shards of coal are reminders of the men who relentlessly toiled here in exchange for scrip, only of value at the company store.

In 0.4 miles, the hiking trail continues straight, where a lightly-used horse trail comes in on your left. Remember this spot, because on your return trip the posted sign makes it easy to get confused. For the next 0.3 miles the hiking trail and the horse trail are one in the same, but the trail is in very good condition and won't cause you any problems. At the next trail junction, the hiking trail bears left and the horse trail continues straight up a rocky hill. This junction is signed with Catawba Overlook to the left and horse trail to your right. It is NOT currently marked for Dick Gap Overlook. You will want to take the horse trail up to Dick Gap Overlook, which is only 0.5 miles, round-trip (despite what many maps say).

Despite it's rocky beginning, the horse trail to the overlook soon levels off and in no time takes you to a gravel turn-around of a dead-end road. Cross the road to pick up the trail on the other side. The overlook has outstanding views of the Blue Heron Mining Camp, the BSF River, and the sandstone bluffs that line the gorge. Return to the main trail and take a right (heading east) on the Kentucky Trail towards the Catawba Overlook.

The Catawba Overlook is a little anti-climatic after Dick's, but you're just getting spoiled, that's all. Just past Catawba there is a seldom-used campsite on your left, atop a small knob, with limited views of the gorge. In fact, all of the campsites along this trail are seldom used and the trails themselves are in very good condition. Most of the day hikers stop at the overlooks or maybe make it all the way to Dick Gap Falls, but that's pretty much it. So it's not unusual to be out here for a few days and not see anyone.

Not long after Catawba Overlook, the canopy becomes increasingly lush and verdant, almost completely blocking out the sunlight. Huge boulders lie scattered along the trail, supporting entire ecosystems of trees, plant life, and little critters. Just after a short ascent, a large rockhouse appears on your right and a double-set of steep wooden stairs leading straight up. Dick Gap Falls is not far beyond this point, off a small spur trail on your left.

Dick Gap Falls only runs during the spring and after heavy rains, but it keeps a small, pleasant trickle year-round. Although the falls itself is less than impressive, the area is really cool with several smaller rockhouses, multitudes of ferns, sandy areas, and quartz pebbles. Dappled shade from the hemlocks and bigleaf magnolias complete the picture. You really do expect to see the little people pop out. Yes, it's worth a visit.

Back on the main trail, turn left and follow the creek drainage towards the river. Once the trees are leafed out, views of the river are infrequent, although you can hear the occasional rapid. From Dick Gap to Big Spring Falls, it's about a mile of easy walking. Along the way you'll cross Big Spring Hollow Creek, which is an excellent place to load up on water. The easiest access point is just before you cross the bridge, on your left.

Continue along the main trail for another 0.15 miles, until you reach the easy spur to the two-tiered Big Spring Falls. The posted sign says 0.3 miles, but that estimation is for out-and-back. This is also a really pretty area, full of rhododendron, mossy rocks, dripping water, and sandy pools. The heavy vegetation makes it difficult to pull off a good photo, but that hasn't stopped many people from trying.

Again, return to the main trail and take another right. From here it's less than 2 miles to Laurel Crossing Branch. The trail slowly climbs out of the gorge, trading evergreens for deciduous trees. At the first field you come to, just hug the tree line on your left to stay on the trail. After 50 or 100 yards, the trail ducks back into the woods before reaching a second field. Here the trail is faint. Head due west for another 100 yards to the opposite tree line and duck back into the woods once again.

There are two camping spots at Laurel Branch. Because of the topography of the BSF, there are limited camping opportunities along the trail and the park service is very generous with their estimation of "legal" campsites. The first campsite is right where the trail begins to follow Laurel Crossing Branch. The second campsite is just before you cross the bridge, up the drainage, and also on your right. Both of these are good places to camp, and the water runs clear and cool. You are only a little over 5 miles from the trailhead, but with all the explorations, it seems a bit longer, in a good way.

If you want to get more mileage in, or stay another night out on the trail, you can continue along the Kentucky Trail to Bald Knob-Hill Cemetery Road, which is a well-maintained gravel lane.

One of the many rock overhangs found along the trail.

Backpacking Kentucky

From Laurel Crossing Branch the trail climbs out of the drainage to more ridgetop hiking. Just past the King Cemetery, turn left on the gravel road and walk 0.1 miles to the Ledbetter Trailhead. Stay straight on the road for another 0.2 miles. Here you will see another small gravel road on your right. This is the horse trail you will be returning on, after completing the loop to the river. From this junction it's another 0.3 miles to where the Kentucky Trail picks up again. (In total, you will have walked 0.6 miles on this gravel road.)

(Note: The Trails Illustrated map does not accurately depict these trail and road intersections. Be sure to carry a copy of the book map provided here.)

Turn right on the Kentucky Trail and hike about a mile down to the river. This is a nice section of old logging road, with few flat camping sites available. Once you hit the river, bear right on the trail. Riverside, there are two camping spots—the first campsite is down a small spur trail on your left that leads to a sandy beach and a small rapid. At high water this campsite may be underwater or no flat spot available. If so, continue down the main trail just a bit more to another campsite in the wooded area on your left. It's always dry here.

Just before Oil Well Branch, the horse trail comes in on your right. If you want to explore a bit, just past the creek is the site of the ca. 1818 Beatty oil well. The site was originally drilled for brine—salt water—but was abandoned shortly after oil starting flowing. At the time, oil (primarily used for medicinal purposes) was less valuable than salt. Imagine that. Since the oil was sold for money, this well is considered the first commercial oil well in the United States. Currently, the well is difficult to find because of dense vegetation, and the chiggers and ticks that hold court there.

Follow the horse trail about 1.3 miles back up to the gravel road. On your left is the smaller Hill Cemetery, filled with babies who died too young and loved ones who will never be forgotten. Turn left on Bald Knob-Hill Cemetery Road. It's 0.2 miles back to the Ledbetter trailhead and 0.1 miles back to the Kentucky Trail. Turn right and find your way back home.

Side Trip: Of course you should explore the Blue Heron Mining Camp, if you have not already done so. The outdoor museum is open seasonally April through October, but the trails are open year-round. Admission to the museum is free.

Freddie the fungus and Alice the algae took a lichen to each other, and soon their relationship ended up on the rocks.
—*ode to Mary Carol Cooper*

Big South Fork National River & Recreation Area:
3. Lick Creek and Princess Falls

The ideal Big South Fork trail--waterfalls, rockhouses, tumbling creeks, and waterfront camping.

Trail Length: 11.7 miles; 20.9 miles if joined with the Yahoo Falls Loop overnighter
Suggested Time: 2 days / 1 night; 3 days / 2 nights
Map: US Forest Service: tinyurl.com/LickCreekTrail

Overview: This overnighter can easily be joined with the Yahoo Falls Loop (the next entry in this book) for a great weekend backpacking trip. Further, this is a great hike any time of the year. Spring rains gather in the creeks producing gorgeous waterfalls. Rock houses stay cool in the heat of summer. Fall brings autumnal colors to the sassafras, beech and oaks. And winter promises icy stalactites and quiet solitude. Just don't tell too many people about this place though. Even a lot of the locals haven't been here.

Directions: From Whitley City, KY turn west on KY 478. Almost immediately, turn left (south) on KY 1651. Drive less than a mile. Turn right on Ranger Station Road (the first paved road past the school bus garage). Parking is immediately on your right, by the kiosk. Trailhead will be on your left, through the Forest Service gate.

Route Description: The first mile of trail follows an old logging road, but this blueberry-laden ridgetop hike won't last long as the trail quickly descends 300 feet into the Lick Creek drainage. Two sets of metal stairs and another 0.25 miles of hiking will bring you to the base of several really nice rockhouses and a seasonal waterfall.

Hiking helps keep life in balance. (K. Rose)

Backpacking Kentucky

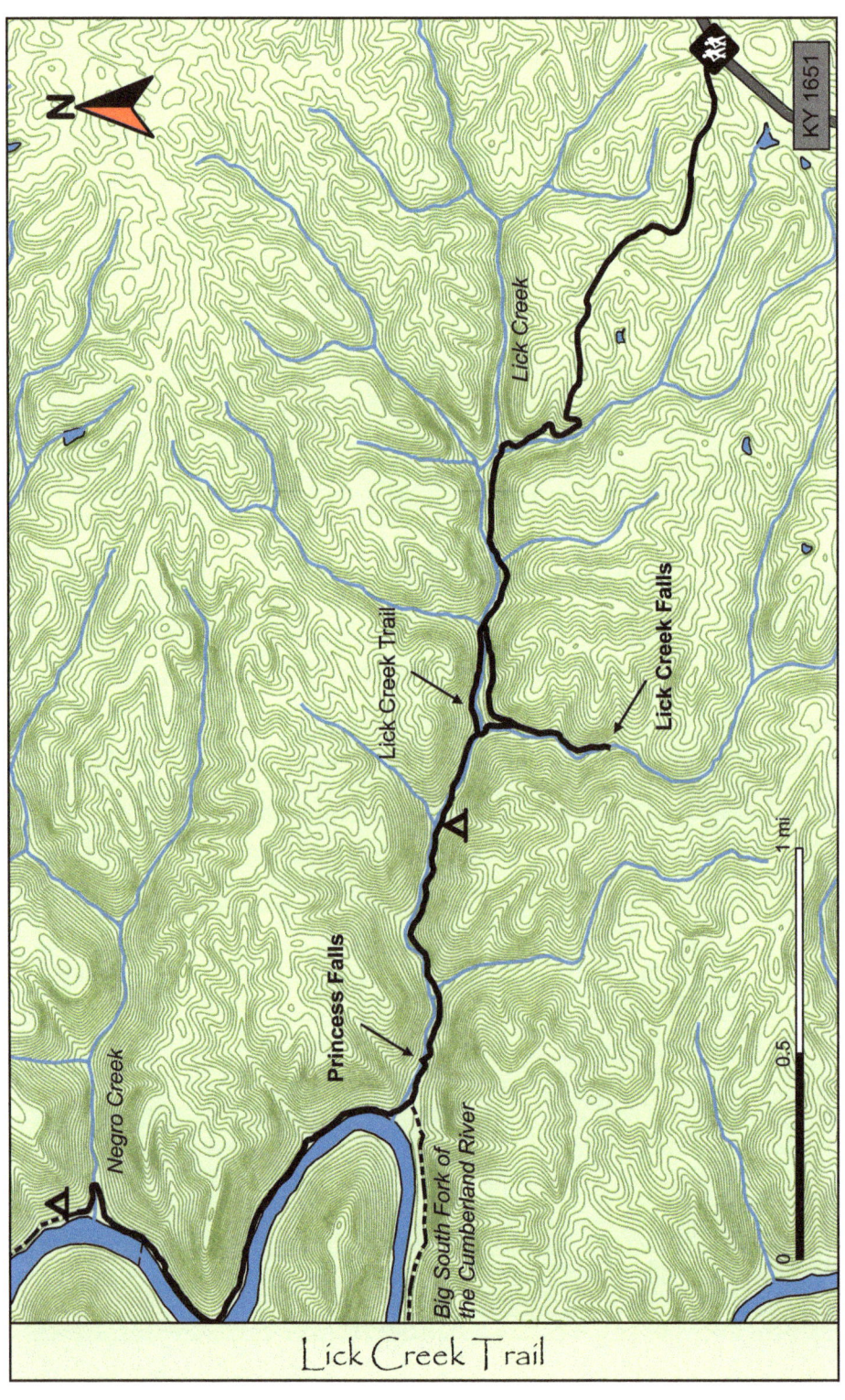

After crossing a small tributary, the trail runs adjacent to Lick Creek. Even at low water levels the two- and three-story boulders lodged in the creek bed create interesting hydraulics and sounds. In the spring, the wildflowers along Lick Creek can be gorgeous. In particular, the area hosts a nice display of lady slippers and mountain laurel.

Winter at Lick Creek Falls. (K. Rose)

Around 2.0 miles from the trailhead, on your left, you will see the 0.5-mile spur to Lick Creek Falls. The trail follows a small tributary of Lick Creek that fools one into underestimating the power and the beauty of the waterfall that lies ahead. Give thanks to the previous trail builders who laid the beautiful stones defining the path as it winds beneath more rock overhangs and shelters. Even in winter, the water seeps and the icicles drip from the huge rock house formed by the falls. A beautiful lunch stop awaits you here at the sand beach formed by the erosion of the rock overhang begun millenniums ago.

Trace your steps back to the main trail, turning left when you rejoin Lick Creek. There is a shortcut down an old trail, but if you're uncertain you can easily backtrack all the way back to the original junction. Either way, bear left (west) on the Lick Creek Trail. Be prepared for several creek crossings, which in early spring can be rather challenging. But remember, the higher the water, the more gorgeous the falls.

In less than 0.5 miles you will pass through a camping area adjacent to the creek. Camping is permitted here, honoring the 25-foot setback from the trail rule. It's possible to set up camp here and day hike to Princess Falls (and Negro Creek if you're so inclined).

Hiking another 0.5 miles or so will lead you to Princess Falls, named after the legendary Cherokee "Princess" Cornblossom. Following the trail on creek-left, you'll see a short spur leading below the waterfall. Whereas Lick Creek Falls is a plunge-style waterfall, Princess is more block-style and forms a curtain as it falls off the bedrock. Even at low water levels, the spring-fed creek continues to create a nice show here and at higher levels Princess Falls is a solid sheet of falling water. Although there is a sweet camping spot just below the falls on creek-right, try and refrain from camping here in order to minimize the visual clutter for other hikers.

Backpacking Kentucky

If you want, continue the last 0.2 miles down Lick Creek Trail to where the trail joins the Sheltowee Trace close to the river. Turning right (north) on the Sheltowee will take you towards the Yahoo area. It's about 1.5 miles from the Lick Creek bridge to Negro Creek and a beautiful double bridge crossing. If you stay on the Sheltowee Trace Trail another 100 yards, there is a large campsite right on the river. This makes for a good overnight spot if you want to stage for the Yahoo Falls Loop the next day.

Side Lore: If you're a sucker for old lore and interesting tidbits, read this. It is recorded that Princess Cornblossom, daughter of Chief Doublehead, was born under the "Sand Cliffs" of Stearns, KY. Princess Cornblossom went on to marry "Big Jake" Troxell, a half-breed Delaware warrior, in Doublehead Cave (located outside of Monticello, KY). After Doublehead was assassinated, Cornblossom became the chief of her tribe. Princess Cornblossom was massacred in 1810 at Yahoo Falls, trying to protect the Chickamauga Cherokee children she was harboring, before taking them to safety at a Presbyterian school in Chattanooga, Tennessee. For more reading, see tinyurl.com/PrincessCornblossom and tinyurl.com/Massacre1810.

Side Trip: After a few days out in the woods, it might feel good to be waited on by someone who smells a little better than you. Check out the Wrigley Taproom and Brewery, 207 S. Main Street in Corbin. Touting 24 rotating craft beers on tap, a multitude of fine bourbons, and a locally-sourced farm-to-table menu, they have quickly gained a loyal following. The burgers and smoked salmon tacos are mighty good eatin'. See their web site for hours and menu at thewrigley.com or call (606) 261–2008.

Not all waterfalls are liquid. (K. Rose)

Big South Fork National River & Recreation Area:
4. Yahoo Falls Loop

The classic Big South Fork backpacking trip.

Trail Length: 9.2 miles; 20.9 miles if joined with the Lick Creek and Princess Falls trip
Suggested Time: 2 days / 1 night; 3 days / 2 nights
Maps: US Forest Service: tinyurl.com/YahooArch
US Forest Service: tinyurl.com/NegroCreek
sheltoweetrace.com/maps/4.pdf

Overview: The Yahoo Falls Loop is the perfect overnighter for those wanting moderate distances. The trail is also a good beginner's trip, with lots of interesting things to see, so you can keep your mind off your back and shoulders. Kids with some backpacking experience will also enjoy the trail. The route takes you clockwise around the loop, although counterclockwise works, too. Highlights include Yahoo Falls, Yahoo Arch, multiple rockhouses and creek drainages, and the Big South Fork of the Cumberland River.

Directions: From Whitley City, KY turn west on KY 700. Drive 4 miles. Turn right on the gravel road, marked for the Yahoo Falls Picnic Area. Drive 1.5 miles to the day-use area. Alternate trailheads include the Alum Ford Campground and where KY 700 crosses the trail.

Staging: If you want to spend the night before hitting the trail, the Sheltowee Trace passes right through Alum Ford Campground. To reach the campground, follow the directions above, but stay on KY 700 until it ends just before the boat ramp. Six primitive sites are located right on the river, available on a first-come, first-served basis. Pit toilets, picnic tables, and bear poles, but no potable water. Just $5 a night. As noted above, you can also make this your starting (and ending) trailhead.

Route Description: The clockwise route combines the Yahoo Arch Trail #602 (2 miles); Negro Creek Trail #612 (2.1 miles); and the Sheltowee Trace Trail #100 (5.1 miles) to form a loop trail. The trail begins at the day-use picnic area for Yahoo Falls. From the far side of the bathrooms, pick up the main trail to Yahoo Falls. There are several small overlooks with views of the river. At 133 feet high, Yahoo Falls is considered the tallest waterfall in Kentucky and beautiful any time of the year. The trail wraps itself around the enormous rockhouse that forms the lip of the falls. A lower trail goes down the center of Yahoo Creek, which if water levels permit, is a totally cool place to explore. There's no hurry here, so take your time exploring the area. Heck, you can even leave your pack in the car and come back for it later.

After exploring the maze of trails found here, head to the far eastern side of the falls area to pick up the trail to Yahoo Arch, which follows the Yahoo Creek drainage. This is one of the best spots for wildflower hunting, while the hemlocks and rhododendron provide a green, lush backdrop year round.

Backpacking Kentucky

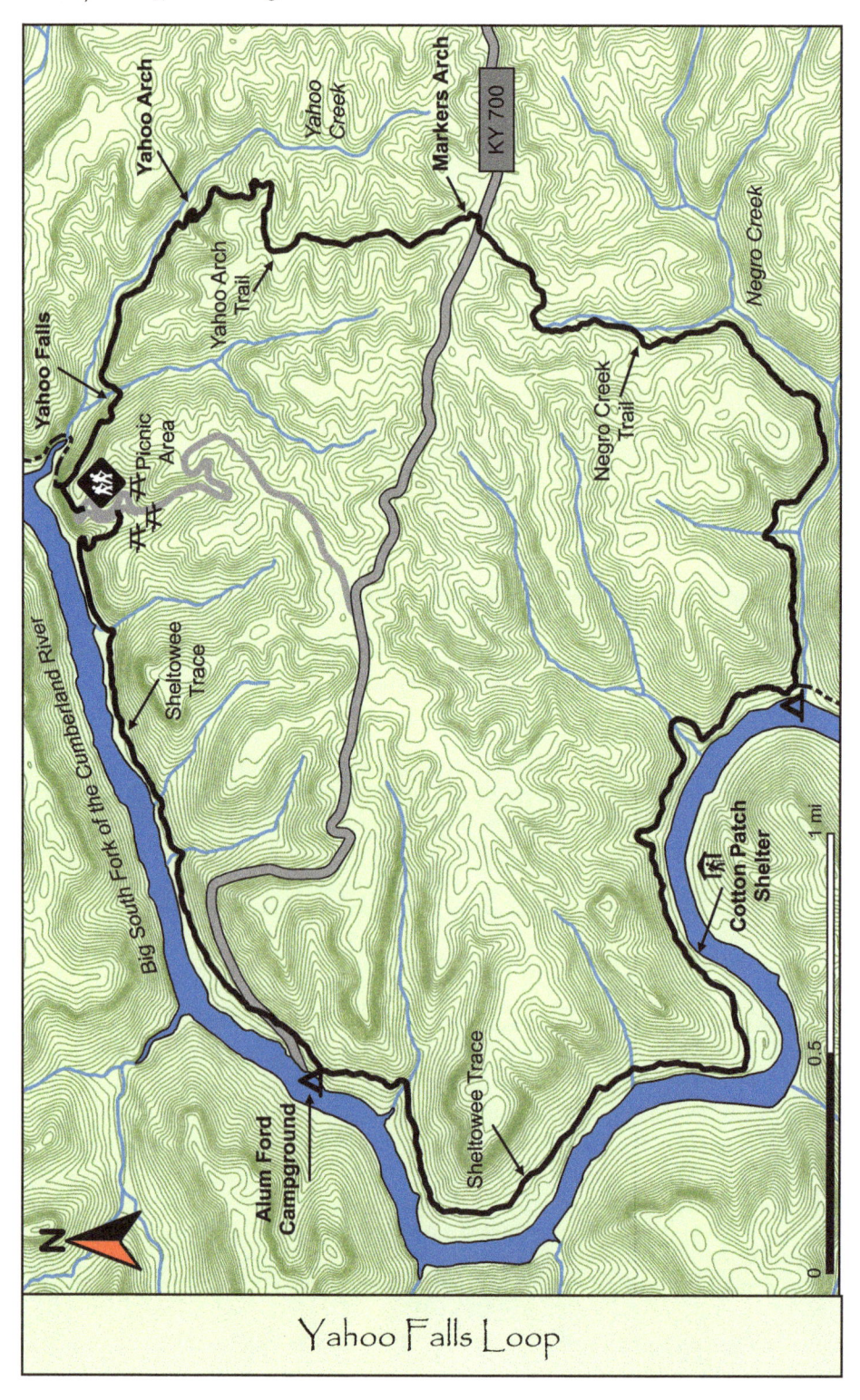

Yahoo Falls Loop

Yahoo Arch is not readily apparent until you nearly fall into the earthen bowl that surrounds this interesting rock structure. One can easily imagine the swirling waters that formed this depression, dissolving the limestone and carving out the sandstone eons ago. The real challenge for modern man is to try and capture all this on your lens.

From here, Yahoo Arch Trail begins a gentle climb along a ridge, before joining an old logging road as it cuts across mountain laurel and wild blueberries. Just before you reach KY 700, you will see a sign on your left for Marker's Arch. While the distance is relatively short (0.5 miles, one-way), the scenery is rather dull and a fallen tree has blocked part of the view of the arch. But if you're notching your belt with arch sightings, this might be worth the detour.

Yahoo Arch Trail ends at KY 700. From here, turn right (west) on the paved highway and make a short dogleg to pick up the 2.1-mile Negro Creek Trail, which begins on the left (south) side of the road. Follow the gated and graveled Forest Service Road 6003 and in only a few yards the trail picks up again. After passing under some power lines, bear right (west) and look for the white diamonds blazing the trail. You'll descend a short section of steps carved into the sandstone, before the trail begins to follow the Negro Creek drainage. Unfortunately, views of the creek are scarce as tits on a boar hog and the sounds of falling water are only apparent after heavy rains.

Negro Creek Trail terminates at the river, where it joins the Sheltowee Trace Trail at a large backcountry camping site. While the camping location is about perfect, the place can get a little worn-looking due to heavy use. But there's a great view of the water, a very large fire pit, and tons of flat places to set up a tent or trees to string a hammock. If you walk upstream on the BSF just a bit and head south on the Sheltowee, there is a really nice set of bridges that cross lovely Negro Creek. It's definitely worth some exploration time.

Large campsite on the BSF River, just north of Negro Creek.

Backpacking Kentucky

Back at the trail junction, head north on the Sheltowee and follow the river downstream. From here, the Sheltowee Trace follows the Big South Fork, passing house-sized boulders, and crossing multiple creeks. About 1.5 miles past the Negro Creek / Sheltowee junction, you'll find a rogue trail off to your left (heading towards the river) leading to the Cotton Patch Shelter (which is not visible from the main trail). If weather is a little sketchy, you might appreciate camping here for the night and having a roof over your head.

Back on the main trail and just past the shelter, you'll see the remains of an old homestead, including a large double-hearth, stone fireplace. Multiple rock fences criss-cross the area, indicating garden patches or livestock pens. If you know the story of this ol' place, I'd love for you to shoot me an email.

Once you reach Alum Ford, the trail passes through the campground. Follow the gravel road to KY 700, bear right and up the hill, and then turn left at the Sheltowee Trace trail sign. You really can't miss it. Duck back into the woods for your last two miles of hiking. This is a pretty stretch of trail, with more house-sized rocks, two small waterfalls, and lots of towering hemlock and rhododendron thickets.

As the trail approaches the Yahoo Falls area, the Sheltowee Trace continues north. Before you climb the stairs to the picnic area, walk just a few more yards to where the Sheltowee crosses over a small bridge amidst several large rockhouses and a seasonal waterfall positioned high up in the drainage. Ooh and ahh, and when you're ready, turn back around and take one step at a time until you get to the Yahoo Falls Day Use Area. The trail emerges close to picnic site #15. Turn left to get back to the bathrooms, or wherever you left your vehicle.

Vanishing points on the trail.

Tip: This trip could easily be an addendum to the Lick Creek and Princess Falls overnighter previously described. Start on the Lick Creek trail until you reach the BSF River, hike the Yahoo Falls Loop, and then return along Lick Creek for a balloon configuration.

Big South Fork

Yahoo Falls is stunning, even at low flow.

Side Trip: After getting off the trail, head back into Whitley City to the Dairy Bar for homemade milkshakes, burgers and pie-in-a-cup, all served in authentic 1950s regalia. They will even take your order outside if you're too dirty or fragrant to be caught on the inside. The Dairy Bar, 198 S. Main Street. (606) 376–2124. Closed on Sundays, but Milton's Burger Hut on US 127 will be open.

Carter Caves State Resort Park:
5. Cross Country Trail

There's plenty of adventure above ground, too.

Trail Length: 8 miles
Suggested Time: 2 days / 1 night
Map: KY State Parks: tinyurl.com/CarterCave

Overview: While most people think of Carter Caves State Park Resort for its below ground activities, that same karst topography that formed the caves has been working above ground to create natural bridges, towering cliffs, and impressive rockhouses and faces. While most of these sights can easily be seen by day hiking, you can turn this into an overnighter by adding on just a bit more mileage.

Directions: From I-64, east of Morehead, take exit #161 at Olive Hill. Turn north on US 60E. Drive 1.4 miles. Turn left on KY 182. Drive 2.7 miles. Cross the bridge over Tygarts Creek and then take an immediate left into the park. Drive a short distance. Turn right into the Welcome Center. Park here or in the overflow parking lot across the road.

Regulations: An overnight permit must be secured from the Welcome Center. Unfortunately there is only one backcountry campsite and they do not take reservations. So you have to risk showing up and keep your fingers crossed that no one has nabbed that permit yet. One good thing is the permit is free. During winter hours, you can pick up the permit from the lodge. Pets are permitted on leash. No open flames.

Staging: At Carter Caves State Resort Park you can opt for a full-service campground, a room at the Lewis Caveland Lodge, or rent a cabin just a short walk from the trailhead. Free backcountry camping is also available at nearby Tygart State Forest.

Route Description: The basic configuration is:
    Carter Caves Cross Country Trail (4Cs)—about 6 miles
    Three Bridges Trail (portion)—2 miles

As soon as you turn into the park entrance, you know this is a special place. Unfortunately, a lot of other people know that too, particularly in summer. So plan your foray accordingly. You can think of this hike for people who want to get away from it all—just not too far away.

Quite honestly, seasoned backpackers would simply do this option as a day hike. But for those wanting to break in some new gear, beginning backpackers, or those with kids, an overnighter at Carter Caves can be a great experience. If you hike this loop counterclockwise, the first day is a little over 5 miles, leaving about 3 miles for day two. Of course, a clockwise rotation would reverse the mileage. The route below assumes you'll travel counterclockwise. Be sure to load up on water before you head out as many creeks run underground after the spring rains let up.

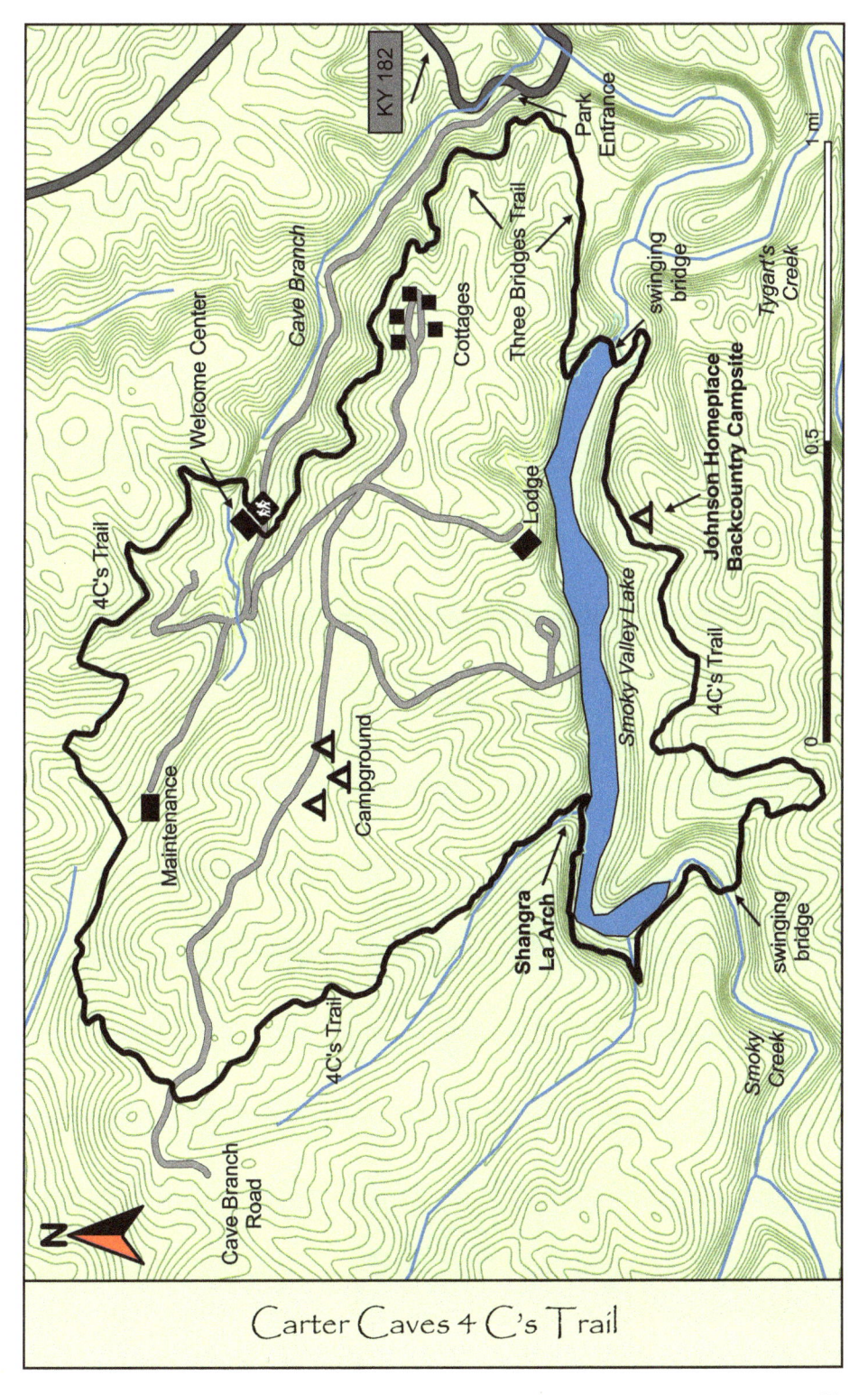

Carter Caves

Carter Caves 4 C's Trail

Backpacking Kentucky

After picking up your permit, head to the far (northeastern) end of the Welcome Center parking lot to get to the trailhead. The trail almost immediately Ys, with the Horn Hollow Trail to your right and the Carter Caves Cross Country Trail (4Cs) to your left. The first thing you'll notice is that the official park map says the 4Cs Trail is 7.5 miles and the sign says 7.2 miles. But it's really closer to 6 miles. And the 4Cs Trail is blazed in orange rectangles and sometimes in yellow CCCC diamonds. Perhaps this is why it's called an "adventure." Regardless, don't worry about counting and just enjoy the ride.

The trail is typically pocked with deer tracks, as the path winds up and down the hilly terrain, passing through hardwood forest. After about 1.25 miles, take a hard right (northwest) onto a service road leading away from the maintenance area. In no time, take a hard left to stay on the 4Cs Trail.

After a short, relentless climb the trail crosses the graveled Cave Branch Road. In about 0.25 miles, the Kiser Hollow Trail splits left and you want to stay right on the 4Cs Trail to Shangra La Arch. Once you reach the arch, stay to the right and look for the steps that lead below the arch. Who thought it was okay to spray paint directions on the stone face? But the creek that originally cut the arch has worked hard to keep up the neighborhood and forms a lovely waterfall just downstream of the arch.

Just past the waterfall, the 4Cs Trail cuts a hard right toward the swinging bridge. Now you are sandwiched between the cliffs on your right and the headwaters of Smoky Valley Lake on your left. The wildflowers in spring are fabulous, but fall is also very rewarding. The next creek crossing also offers a nice waterfall, on its way to cutting a new arch for the next millennials to enjoy.

In no time, you'll be crossing Smoky Creek on the swinging bridge. This is a really pretty place, so take your time and rest up before your next climb. In less than a mile you will see the "old Johnson Homeplace," which is marked by daffodils in springtime, an old stone chimney year-round, and bits of broken crockery and colored glass. The campsite is not marked, so you'll have to look for the flat worn spot used by all the backpackers before you.

The next morning, you have about 0.5 miles of hiking before you begin to see the large earthen berm that contains the lake. Your goal is to get to the other side of the tailwater—and good luck to you! The trail gets lost here, as water levels fluctuate throughout the year, leaving behind a trail of detritus.

Reaching for the light.

Pick your way about and look for the really cool bridge that crosses the tailwater itself. Beyond the bridge, bear left to stay on the 4Cs Trail, hug the base of the cliff, and head up the stairs until you T into the Three Bridges Trail.

Bear right (due east) for the quickest way back to the trailhead. The Three Bridges Trail is one of the best in the park, so enjoy all the rockhouses, particularly Fern Bridge and the overhead arch. You have about 2 miles to go before you reach the Welcome Center.

Side Trip: There are lots of other sights to see above and below ground at Carter Caves State Resort Park. Above ground, Smoky Bridge, Natural Bridge, and the Box Canyon Trail are all worth checking out.

Looking up from Fern Bridge.

Cave Run Lake

The state of Kentucky and the US Army Corps of Engineers went wild during the 1960s and '70s, damming most of the major rivers in the state with the purpose of reducing downstream flooding, providing water-based recreational activities, and in some cases, generating electricity. The damming of the Licking River achieved the first two of those goals by creating Cave Run Lake. While the Corps still manages the lake and its shoreline, Cave Run itself lies within the Daniel Boone National Forest.

The Forest Service recently evaluated all of the trails in the Cave Run Lake area. As a result of this new management plan, many hiking trails are no longer maintained and connectors have been eliminated. In tandem, new horse, ATV and mountain biking trails are being developed. Although hikers are allowed on all of these trails, the backpacking recommendations in this book favor trails geared toward hikers. In addition, many maps are no longer accurate. The link provided below will lead you to the updated Forest Service map.

You can hike these trails in the spring for the wildflowers, during the dog days of summer for the swimming, or in the fall for the magnificent colors. But the lake views are most prominent when the leaves are off the trees.

Regulations: All foodstuffs and garbage must be stored in a bear-resistant container or properly suspended at least ten feet clear of the ground at all points, suspended at least four feet horizontally from the supporting tree or pole, and suspended at least four feet from any other tree or pole adjacent to the supporting tree or pole (per US Forest Service regulations).

If considering the Buckskin options, several of the trails in the Cave Run Lake area also lie within the Pioneer Weapons Wildlife Management Area. You may want to check the timing of various hunting seasons by going to the Kentucky Department of Fish and Wildlife Resources web page at fw.ky.gov.

Cave Run Lake:
6. Caney Loop Trail

An easy hike with waterfront campsites.

Trail Length: 8.5 miles
Suggested Time: 2 days / 1 nights
Map: US Forest Service: tinyurl.com/CaveRun

Overview: The trail starts near the dam at Cave Run Lake, which impounds the Licking River. The loop can be hiked either direction, or even done as an out-and-back if you want to stay lakeside. While the summer promises wonderful swimming opportunities, hiking the trail in late spring or early fall are both excellent choices.

Directions: From I-64, just west of Morehead, KY, take the Sharkey/Farmers exit #133. Turn south on KY 801. Drive for 5.1 miles. Turn right on KY 826. Drive 0.8 miles, crossing over the dam, until you see the left-hand turn for the Stoney Cove Recreation Area. You'll want to park in the far gravel lot on your left, just past the kiosk. No parking pass is required.

Staging: You can camp in the Twin Knobs Campground, just a bit further south on KY 801. Open seasonally.

Route Description: From the parking lot, follow the gravel service road that goes behind the kiosk. Just up the small hill, the loop begins with the "new" Sheltowee Trace trail #100 leading to your left and the Caney Trail #1226 to your right. It use to be the other way around…but in late summer 2016 the Forest Service rerouted the Sheltowee Trace onto the lakeside of the loop. Nonetheless, most people just refer to this hike as the Caney Loop. And while other camping sites can be found in the interior of the loop, why not have beach front property?

Most people hike this loop clockwise, bearing left at the aforementioned intersection onto the Sheltowee Trace trail #100. Passing beneath a canopy of maples, oaks, and sons of birches and beeches, the trail begins to hug the shoreline of the lake. In about 2.0 miles, the trail follows Caney Creek, a tributary popular among fishermen and boaters alike. The trail remains wide and fairly flat with gentle undulations caused by seasonal creek drainages. About 4.0 miles from the trailhead is a nice lunch spot, complete with logs to sit on, and a fire pit for those sausages stashed in your pack.

The Sheltowee crosses under some power lines about 5.6 miles from the trailhead and joins the Caney Trail #1226 at around 5.75 miles. A left (west) turn here would take you to the White Sulphur Horse Camp and a right (east) turn takes you onto #1226. So bear right to continue your clockwise rotation. Another 2.5 miles of hiking on #1226 and you'll be back to the Stoney Cove parking lot. As a reminder—if by chance you encounter some horseback riders, please step off the trail and let them have the right-away.

Backpacking Kentucky

Caney Loop Trail

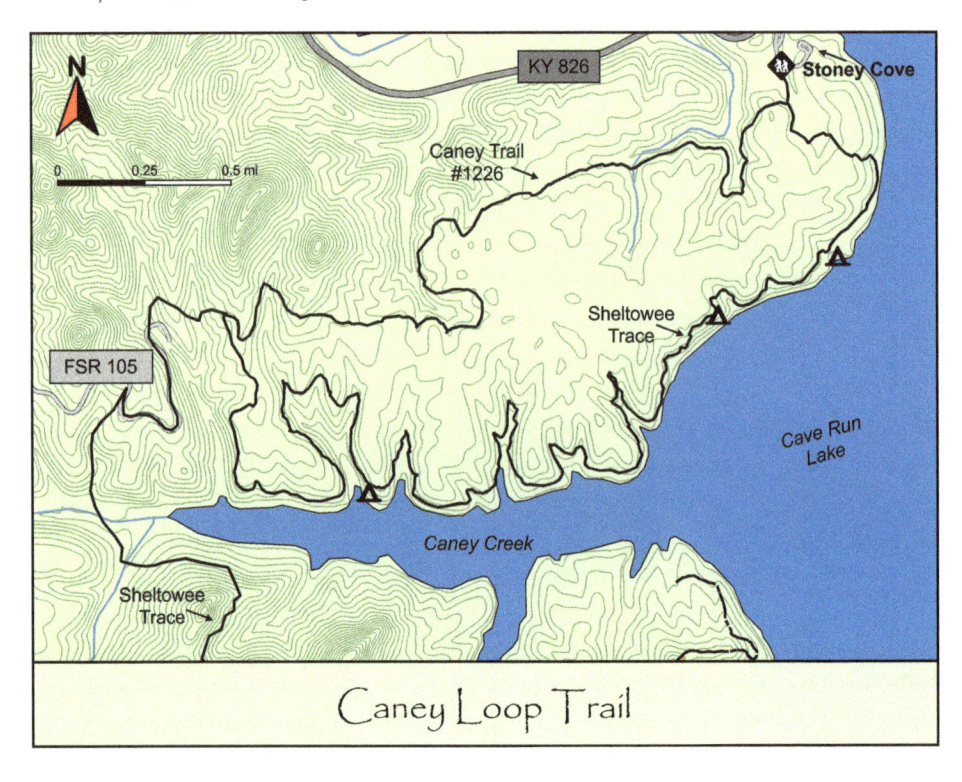

Side Trips: After backpacking, you may want to head over to the Minor E. Clark Fish Hatchery that you passed on KY 801, just north of the dam. The hatchery is quite an interesting place to poke around if you have some extra time. Free tours are available.

Then stop by Pop's Southern Style BBQ at the corner of KY 801 and US 60, heading back to the interstate. This little joint is a small mammal, taxidermist's delight. Grab a plate of mouth-watering pulled pork and hot, fresh cobbler as squirrels and possums serenade you on miniature banjos.

Squawroot or bear corn, a non-photosynthesizing parasitic plant.

Cave Run Lake:
7. Buckskin Trail

Lots of different trail configurations are possible to combine creekside walking and ridgetop hiking, all leading to campsites along the shores of Cave Run Lake.

Trail Length: 13.7 to 19.4 miles, with shorter options available
Suggested Time: 2 days / 1 night; 3 days / 2 nights
Map: US Forest Service: tinyurl.com/CaveRun

Overview: You have lots of different backpacking options here, but the two best choices are both lollipop trail configurations. The first option starts from the Zilpo TH of the Buckskin Trail, close to Zilpo Campground. The trail follows the shoreline of Cave Run Lake for most of the way before looping interior along Cave Run Trail and following Big Cave Run creek back to the Buckskin Trail for a 13.7-mile trip.

The second option starts at the Clear Creek Trailhead. This trail is more of a roller coaster ride, climbing up sharp ridges, before descending back to creekside again. Highlights include the Tater Knob Fire Tower. Same as option one, the Buckskin Trail takes backpackers to the shoreline of Cave Run Lake, with plentiful water and swimming opportunities.

Important Note: A 3.4-mile section of the Buckskin Trail (marked in orange on the accompanying map) is frequently closed from Dec. 1 through July 1 due to eagle nesting activity. Please route your trip with this in mind. Although the campsites directly across the lake from Twin Knobs Campground are not available during these months, the two campsites at the far northern end of the map are always open. You can call the US Forest Service at (606) 784–6428 to get current trail conditions.

Directions: From I-64, west of Morehead, KY, take the Owingsville/Salt Lick exit #123. Turn right on US 60. Drive 6.6 miles. Turn right on KY 211 and take the dogleg through the town of Salt Lick. Drive another 3.7 miles. Turn left on Clear Creek Road (KY 129). You should see a sign for the Zilpo Recreational Area. Go another 4.0 miles and then follow the directions below.

To Zilpo Trailhead: Turn left on KY 918 (Zilpo National Forest Scenic Byway, aka Zilpo Road) toward Zilpo Campground. You'll see a sign for the Pioneer Weapons Hunting Area immediately on your right. Drive 8.0 miles. Turn left at the sign for the Buckskin Trailhead. The small gravel road will lead you to a parking loop. The trailhead is on the west side of the parking area.

To Clear Creek Trailhead: Instead of turning left on KY 918 toward the Zilpo Campground, stay straight on Leatherwood Road (KY 129). Drive 2 more miles (or about 1 mile past the Glady primitive camping area). Park in the small gravel area on your right where FS Road #915 is gated before crossing the creek. This is the trailhead for both the Cave Run Lake Trail

#116 and the Leatherwood Loop Trail #116A. Do not block the gate. The trailhead is on the north (opposite) side of the paved road.

Staging: For the Zilpo TH option: There is a great lakeshore campsite about 0.35 miles from the parking area. Or you can camp at Zilpo Campground, but reservations are recommended on holiday weekends and during the summer. You can also camp at Clear Creek Campground (see below).

For the Clear Creek TH option: Before you get to the Clear Creek TH, you will pass Clear Creek Campground, run by the US Forest Service. It has 21 unimproved sites, which includes potable water and pit toilets, but no hook-ups. There's a really interesting stone "iron furnace" in the picnic area. The campground is open mid-April through November. Further down the road, you will pass several backcountry campsites along Leatherwood Creek. They can get a little trashed, but they're free.

Route Description: Option #1 Zilpo Trailhead: 13.7 miles
Buckskin Trail #113—7 miles
Cave Run Trail #112—2.9 miles
Connector Trail #108—0.2 miles
Return on Buckskin #113—3.6 miles

The Buckskin Trail leads from the west side of the parking loop. After a brief descent, the path quickly comes to a T, with the right-hand heading towards Zilpo Campground. Your boots want to turn left here, to follow the Buckskin Trail along the lakeshore. The trail is randomly blazed with yellow and white diamonds. The first campsite, complete with an excellent pebble beach for swimming and beautiful spots for a campfire, is about 0.35 miles from the parking lot and down a short path to the water's edge.

Unfortunately floodwaters of previous years have washed up some detritus along this section of the trail. Although the decomposition rates of glass and Styrofoam will leave us all in the dust, nature is quickly reclaiming her own.

For the next 3+ miles, the Buckskin Trail weaves in and out of small drainages, none of which hold much water from late spring to early fall. But the path remains shaded all summer long and the fall colors are brilliant. As the spring flowers fade, be on the lookout for the myriad colorful mushrooms that inhabit these deciduous woods.

Shortly after the trail begins paralleling Big Cave Run creek, make a sharp right to cross the creek and hike the lollipop portion of the trail counter-clockwise. At this junction you'll see a sign reading 'Cave Run Trail – Foot Travel Only.' This is where you will return to the Buckskin at the end of the loop portion of this hike. After crossing the creek, you will see another sign and just beyond it the trail weaves between two small, cut logs. While the minutiae of detail? Because shortly the trail will bear left and not straight as one might think, so keep an eye out.

So bear left here and in another 0.1 miles there is a decent campsite on your right. In spring the surrounding area can become rather boggy, as you are within the flood plain of the creek. You might want to look for higher ground if you plan on spending the night here.

The Buckskin Trail then makes a steep ascent for about 0.5 miles before hitting the Hog Pen Trail, which is really FR 1225. If the Buckskin is closed for eagle nesting activity, you'll have to bear left here. Otherwise bear right on #113, which leads to a small

Cave Run Lake

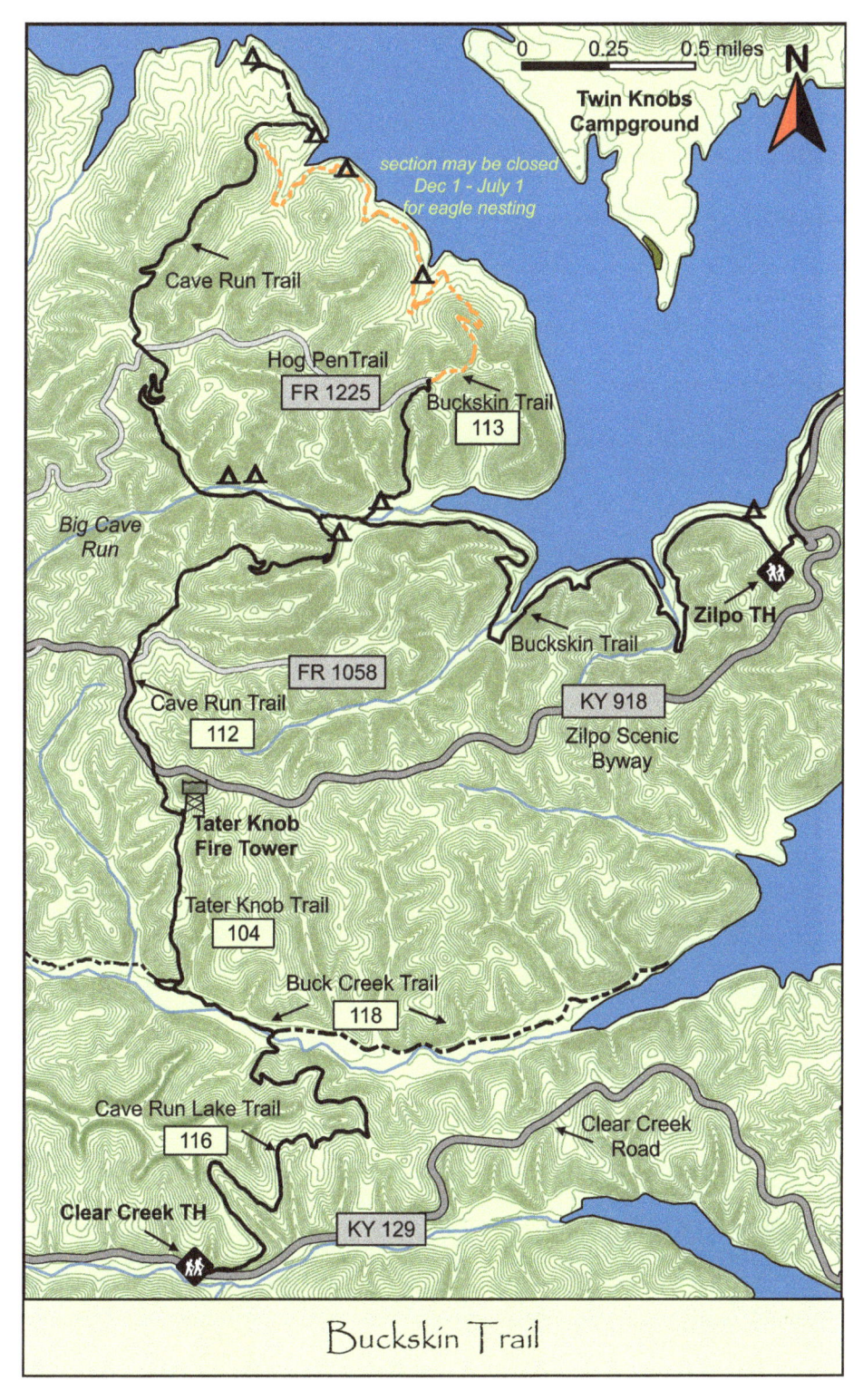

Buckskin Trail

meadow and sharp ridge line, before descending a set of switchbacks back down toward the lake. While you can camp up here, there is no water available except for a small, cattail and frog-filled pond.

At the bottom of this descent, the trail drops into a small drainage with a campsite on your right that has limited lake access. If you are continuing on the trail, bear left here to hike a little further up into the drainage, before crossing the small creek, and following the trail down the other side.

Continuing along the Buckskin, the next campsite has a small trail that leads to another pebble beach. Shade is plentiful here, but lots of sunny patches persist along the shoreline. There's even a clothesline and pins to hang your birthday suit after skinny-dipping your way into evening. Relaxing on the beach and star-gazing at night might be on your agenda.

About a mile from here, the Buckskin Trail joins with the Cave Run Trail (#112). At one time in very recent memory, the trail continued all the way along the shoreline until it met up with the Sheltowee Trace. But this section of trail is no longer maintained. However, there are a few good campsites out on this north-facing point of land with lots of shade, fire pits, and easy access to the lake.

Continuing on the loop, the Cave Run Trail ascends for about 2.0 miles, before reaching the Hog Pen Trail at ridgetop. Camping is limited here and water difficult to come by. After crossing the Hog Pen, take #112 back down to Big Cave Run creek. There are a few camping spots along the creek, but not as many as one might hope. Although the creek dries up considerably in late summer, in spring this section of the trail has some of the best wildflowers in the area.

The Connector Trail #108 brings you once again to the Buckskin Trail. Stay straight and make your way back to the trailhead. You can easily drive to the Tater Knob Fire Tower on the way back and hike a short distance to see this piece of valuable history and admire the views.

Option #2 Clear Creek Trailhead: 19.4 miles
- Cave Run Lake Trail #116—2.8 miles
- Buck Creek Trail #118—0.5 miles
- Tater Knob Trail #104—1.0 mile
- Cave Run Trail #112—1.9 miles
- Connector Trail #108—0.2 miles
- Buckskin Trail #113—3.4 miles
- Cave Run Trail #112—5.3 miles
- Tater Knob Trail #104—1.0 mile
- Buck Creek Trail #118—0.5 miles
- Cave Run Lake Trail #116—2.8 miles

The hike described below is also a lollipop configuration, stringing together almost every trail in the immediate area. No quilt has a better patchwork pattern than this hike. So grab a good map and compass, and let's go.

Begin by crossing back over KY 129 and heading north on the Cave Run Lake Trail (#116). In 2.8 miles you'll climb up towards what is known as Chestnut Cliffs, wrap around the far eastern side, then descend 300 vertical feet to where the Cave Run Lake Trail crosses Buck Creek and Ts into the Buck Creek Trail (#118). Immediately on the other side of the creek, turn left (west) on #118 and hike about 0.5 miles. Just past a small wet-weather stream, you should see Tater Knob Trail (#104) come in on your right.

Turn right (east, then north) on #104 for a steep 1.0-mile or 600 vertical feet ascent to the base of the old Tater Knob Fire Tower. Built in 1934 by the Civil Conservation Corps, the tower is on the National Historic Lookout Register. Unfortunately the wooden structure of the tower was destroyed by arson in 2008—and with it the fabulous views afforded to anyone who would dare climb its steps. But the remaining metal frame is quite interesting and the views are still stunning. Furthermore, the good news is that funds have been secured to rebuild the tower sometime in the near future. Be sure to climb up to the base of the tower, which provides 360-degree views of the surrounding ridgetops. Although the tower is but a shell of its former glory, at the top you'll soar with the ravens as they climb the thermals.

Just west of the tower, Tater Knob Trail joins with Cave Run Trail #112 and crosses over a paved road (KY 918). The trail parallels the eastern side of the road for about 0.4 miles, while continuing to head north. Just where the trail departs from the road's shoulder, bear right (northeast) on FR #1058, then left to continue along Cave Run Trail (#112). (Cave Run Trail versus Cave Run Lake Trail. Isn't that just confusing? You would think they could have come up with more original names.)

Tater Knob Fire Tower.

Follow Cave Run Trail #112 for about 1.5 miles, the last section being a set of switchbacks as you climb back down the ridge into the Peter Cave Run and Big Cave Run drainages. There are several good places to camp along Big Cave Run creek. To hike the lollipop counter-clockwise, turn right (east) on a short 0.2-mile connector trail that will take you to the Buckskin Trail (#113). (There! They did it again! Buck Creek versus Buckskin trails.)

Be sure to water up here before turning left (northeast) on the Buckskin Trail. Once again you have a sharp ascent, climbing 400 vertical feet over 0.8 miles. Stay right on #113, where the Hog Pen Trail comes in on your left. There are a couple of good camping spots along this section, but no water at hand.

Almost all of your hiking on the Buckskin Trail follows the contours of the lake. Both campsites marked on the accompanying map are good ones, with water and swimming available. Bald eagles frequent this area, so be on the lookout. Across the lake you will see Twin Knobs Campground and its two namesakes.

Backpacking Kentucky

Staying on the Buckskin, you will see Cave Run Trail #112 reappear on your left. The Buckskin Trail use to continue here and is still easy to follow. There are 2-3 good campsites at the far north end of the accompanying map, with easy water access and more swimming opportunities. The trail system use to connect all the way over to the Sheltowee Trace and the dam at Stoney Cove, but this portion of the trail is no longer being maintained.

To complete the lollipop, head up the hill on the Cave Run Trail #112. You'll need to climb for about 1.5 miles before reaching the junction of Cave Run, Hog Pen and Cross Over trails. Stay on Cave Run Trail for another 1.5 miles, until you get back to Big Cave Run Creek. Hike downstream along the creek for about 0.4 miles (again, with some good camping opportunities). Bear right at the Connector Trail junction to stay on the Cave Run Trail and hike back to Tater Knob. Retrace your steps back to your vehicle using the Tater Knob, Buck Creek, and Cave Run Lake trails. Your last turn will be right on the Cave Run Lake Trail #116, and you're 2.8 miles from your vehicle.

Camping near the Zilpo Trailhead.

Other Options: Starting near the Tater Knob fire tower or the trailhead on FS Road #1058 can significantly shorten this route.

Side Trip: Remember driving past Clear Creek Market? On your way home, be sure to grab a piece of pie in this cafe and general store. Ooh la la... chocolate peanut butter pie. Their homemade pies are worth every calorie you just burned. Heck. They'll even sell you the whole pie.

Cumberland Gap National Historic Park:
8. Ride the Ridge Trail to the Hensley Settlement

A challenging hike atop Cumberland Mountain, with lots to see and do.

Trail Length: 20+ miles one-way (40+ miles, round-trip)
Suggested Time: 3 days / 2 nights (4 days / 3 nights)
Maps: National Park Service: tinyurl.com/CumbGap
    OutrageGIS.com

Overview: The Boy Scouts call this trail the Mischa Mokwa. For history buffs, it celebrates the famous road through Cumberland Gap. For those who lived high on the ridge, it was a way of life. For backpackers…well, it's just darn challenging. But exploring the Hensley Settlement, Sand Cave, and White Rocks, makes this trail an adventure worth living.

Directions: From Middlesboro, KY, take US 25 E into the Cumberland Gap Historical National Park. The Visitor Center will be on your right. Back on US 25 E, the highway passes through Cumberland Gap Tunnel as you cross into the Volunteer State. After the tunnel, stay in the right lane to follow US 58 E into Virginia. Drive about 2 miles. Turn left on National Park Road, following the signs to the Wilderness Road Campground. Drive 1.0 mile. Free overnight parking is available across from the campground office.

Regulations: All backcountry camping must be in one of the five designated campsites. Permits are required (free) and must be picked up in person at the Visitor Center. Backcountry permits can be reserved up to three months in advance. To make reservations, call the park visitor center at (606) 248–2817. The Martins Fork cabin is also available and features a large stone fireplace, three wood bunk beds, front and back porches, and a picnic table. Cost is $10 per night. Advance reservations can be made using the same number above.

All food and garbage must be stored in bear canisters (vaults) or properly hung. Cables with hooks are provided at each of the designated campsites. Although (surprisingly) several of the cable systems violate the recommended set-back distance to the campsites, they are easy to use.

Staging: A full-service campground, Wilderness Road, is located at the trailhead.

Route Description: Mileage below does not include sightseeing at the Hensley Settlement or the spur to Martins Fork.
    Wilderness Road Campground to Gibson Gap Campsite—5.1 miles
    Gibson Gap Campsite to Hensley Camp—6.2 miles
    Hensley to White Rocks—5.5 miles (includes spur to Sand Cave)
    White Rocks to Walker Civic Park—3.2 miles

Backpacking Kentucky

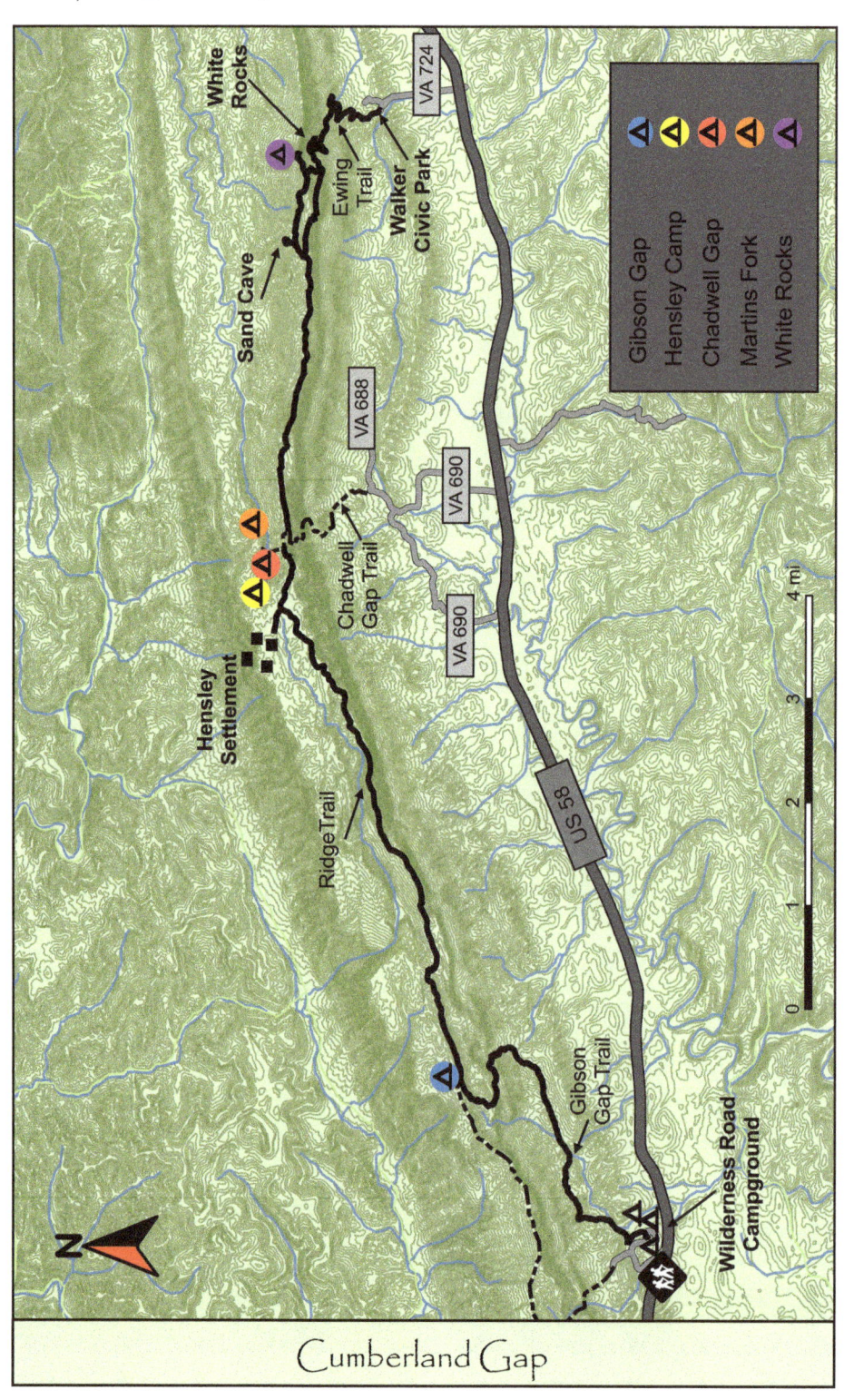

46

Cumberland Gap

There are lots of ways to skin this cat, but one of the best is to start at the Wilderness Road Campground, hike the Gibson Gap Trail up to the Ridge Trail, head east towards the Hensley Settlement, and then hit Sand Cave and White Rocks on your way out the Ewing Trail. This requires running a shuttle, but it's less than 20 minutes one-way from the campground to the Thomas Walker Civic Park (basically stay on US 58 E, then hang a left on VA 724.)

Others prefer hiking the full Ridge Trail leaving from the Pinnacle Overlook (which provides views of KY, VA and TN all from one vantage point), thereby avoiding the Gibson Gap Trail. Leaving from the Pinnacle Overlook is nearly identical mileage, but allows you to miss most of the uphill to the ridgetop since you are driving to the pinnacle. But the Gibson Gap Trail is preferred if you really want to feel the burn of the climb, making victory that much sweeter—so that's the way the hike is described below.

After running shuttle and leaving your pick-up vehicle at Civic Park, begin from the Wilderness Road Campground. There is free overnight parking across from the park office, found in several diagonal parking slots. From here, follow the Greenleaf Nature Trail (and/or the Honey Tree Spur Nature Trail) and make your way over to the Gibson Gap Trail. Although you should have permit in hand, go ahead and sign in on the hiker's log.

The first few miles of the Gibson Gap Trail is literally a walk in the park. Hiking is pleasant. Hiking is flat. Views are scenic enough. But about halfway into your hike, the trail bears left up a steep hill (don't be tempted to remain a lowlander by staying along the creek side.) Here the going gets a little tougher as you follow in the steps of Dr. Thomas Walker, a physician from Virginia and early explorer extraordinaire. Walker is credited with "discovering" Cumberland Gap in 1750, which was not blazed by Daniel Boone until 15 years later. Story has it that Walker, his comrades, and a group of Indians were passing through a noteworthy gap, found a sweet little spring, passed a bottle of rum, and toasted the Duke of Cumberland. And history beats on.

The Gibson Gap Campsite is found where the trail terminates with the Ridge Trail. If 5+ miles is a good day for you and you have permit in hand, this makes a good spot for the first night. The site is large and somewhat flat, with a fire pit and cable/hook system to hang food. If you follow the Ridge Trail west and walk about 50-100 yards down the hill, there is a small spring and beginnings of a creek where you can obtain water. Notably, up on the ridge it is several degrees cooler than down in the valley.

To reach the Hensley Settlement, continue east along the Ridge Trail. From here you have 6+ miles to the next designated campsite. The Ridge Trail essentially forms the state border between Kentucky (on your left or north side of the trail) and Virginia (on your right or south side of the trail). The trail along this section is

At the top. Victory is sweet! (B. Askren)

Backpacking Kentucky

fairly wide and rolling, with occasional views of the valley as you look south. In mid-summer, may of these views are obstructed from the tree canopy overhead.

After about 6 miles, the Ridge Trail dips down, crosses a small creek, ascends once again and comes to a T. This creek is important because it is your water source for the next two designated campsites. At the T, a left (northwesterly) turn will take you to the Hensley Settlement and a right (southeasterly) turn takes you first to the Hensley Camp and then to the Chadwell Gap campsites (each on your left).

Although both of these campsites are fine for an overnighter, the Hensley Camp is closer to the creek and the settlement, quite large with lots of good flat spots, a big fire pit surrounded with logs to sit upon, and a cable/hook system for hanging food just on the other side of the trail. However, this campsite is also immediately adjacent to the trail. The Chadwell Gap Campsite is a short distance further down the Ridge Trail and has complete privacy—but has very few flat spots and is further from both the creek and the settlement.

If you're willing to walk a tad bit further (maybe 0.5 miles), the Martins Fork Campsite has a lot to offer. It is extremely private, has a sweet little cabin, a large grassy field to set up tents and trees for hammocks, and is on Martins Fork, which serves as your water supply. Even if you don't rent the cabin, the front and back porches are great places to hang out and get out of the rain, if necessary.

Camping at any of these three campsites gives you good access to the Hensley Settlement, an early 1900s homestead community comprised of the Hensley and Gibbons families. You can easily spend a couple of hours roaming the meadows, peering into the windows of the chestnut-hewn log cabins and old school, exploring the barns and chicken coops, reading the tombstones, and looking for the bootlegger's operation. Unfortunately the signage is almost non-existent as the Park Service conducts tours up here from late spring to mid-fall. But to hook up with a tour, you need to start at the Visitors Center. It's a conspiracy! Nonetheless, be sure to reserve a nice chunk of time for the Hensley Settlement. There are bathrooms at the far eastern side and potable water from an outdoor spigot located near the maintenance building.

Life at the Hensley Settlement. (B. Askren)

Cumberland Gap

From the campsites, it's about 4 miles to Sand Cave, a humongous rockhouse about 250 feet across and looming over 1.25 acres of sand. Absolutely don't miss the short spur trail that drops down to a beautiful little creek, leading to a waterfall and the rockhouse. You can easily spend an hour here exploring the area.

Sand Cave—Beach volleyball anyone? (B. Askren)

From Sand Cave, it's less than a mile to White Rocks, a massive limestone outcropping that towers 2000 feet above the valley floor below. The views all face Virginia, with lots of places to lose loved ones if you're not careful. Again, be sure to budget enough time here to enjoy the sights.

From the White Rocks area, you have about a 3.2-mile hike down the Ewing Trail to get to the Walker Civic Park. The park has restrooms, picnic tables, and a shelter. Pick up your shuttle vehicle and drive back to the Wilderness Road Campground.

Side Trip: Of course, if you have the time, buying a seat on the tour bus to the Hensley Settlement is an option. But at this point, it might feel a little bit like cheating. The drive to the Pinnacle Overlook, at the far western end of the park is also quite scenic, with excellent views of Kentucky, Tennessee and Virginia.

Land Between the Lakes

The Land Between the Lakes National Recreation Area (LBL), encompassing 170,000 acres of forest, wetlands, and open meadows, lies in far western Kentucky. Nestled between Kentucky Lake to the west and Lake Barkley to the east, LBL has over 500 miles of trails available for hiking, backpacking, horseback riding, and mountain biking. Select trails are also open for ATV use.

Kentucky Lake was formed when the Tennessee Valley Authority impounded the Tennessee River in the 1940s for the production of hydro-electric power. Twenty years later the US Corps of Engineers impounded the Cumberland River, creating Lake Barkley. The two reservoirs are linked at their northern-most reaches by a narrow canal, allowing barges and pleasure craft to travel between the two lakes. The Tennessee River flows into the Ohio River, just a few miles further north.

With an additional 220,000 water acres and 300 miles of natural shoreline, LBL offers excellent opportunities for boating enthusiasts and freshwater anglers. Crappie, bass, bluegill, and sauger fishing is deemed some of the best in the state.

Camping is available year-round, with 4 developed campgrounds, 14 backcountry sites with lake access, and 3 primitive sites. Other park attractions include the Golden Pond Planetarium, Woodlands Nature Station, Elk & Bison Prairie, and the Homeplace 1850s Working Farm and Living History Museum.

View of Kentucky Lake from the North/South Trail.

Hunting is also popular at LBL, with the usual variety of archery, crossbow, and gun seasons for deer, turkey, small animal, and waterfowl. Trapping is also permitted per regulations. Please see the LBL web site (www.landbetweenthelakes.us) or call the visitor center at (800) 525–7077 to learn about current hunting seasons.

Land between the Lakes has hundreds of miles of trail. But the only trails suitable for backpacking are the Canal Loop Trail (an 11-mile loop); the North/South Trail–North End (31 miles one-way); and the North/South Trail–South End (27 miles one-way); and the Fort Henry Trails (30 miles of various configurations).

The Canal Loop Trail is presented here as an easy overnighter and for kids in Part 2 of the book. The trail is extremely popular amongst mountain bikers, but they are very accommodating to hikers—with the possible exception of race days.

The North/South Trail is also a multi-use trail. Hikers and mountain bikers share the North End of the trail, while the South End is open to hikers and horseback riders. The trail is blazed in white diamonds (or rectangles in places); connector trails and springs are blazed with yellow diamonds.

Backcountry camping is also permitted in the Fort Henry Trail system. However, some of the trails are currently closed and lake access is extremely limited. But don't rule out some of the most beautiful trails in the park that are found here.

Ticks are a problem in LBL, so be prepared with long pants and shirt sleeves, insect repellent, and a constant vigilance. Treating your hiking clothing in advance with a Permethrin product (found in farm supply stores and some outfitters) can work wonders.

The best time to hike the trails is spring or fall, as summer gets too hot and humid, and winters can be brutal with westerly winds blowing off Kentucky Lake. In spring, water is plentiful along the trails, but heavy rains can limit camping options along the low-lying areas and the shorelines. Fall presents other challenges as almost all creeks dry up and many hunters do not obey the minimum 150-yard set-back requirement from "any developed anything" including roads, trails, and camping areas. But on the plus-side, cooler fall weather brings a huge decline in the tick population. And the autumn colors contrast beautifully with the deep blue hue of the lakes.

Regulations: LBL distinguishes between *backcountry camping* and *backpacking*. If you are parking your vehicle and carrying your gear to a backcountry site, you need a "Backcountry Camping Permit" which costs $30 per year or $7 for a 3-day permit.

But if you are simply backpacking, all you need is a free "Backpacking Permit," which is available at the North Welcome Station, the Golden Pond Visitor Center, and the South Welcome Station. Backpacking permits can be picked up after hours at the self-serve kiosk at each location and on-line.

Campsites must be 50 feet from the trail. Human waste should be buried 200 feet from the trail. All pets must be on a 6-foot leash or less, and must be under physical control at all times. Only build fires in pre-existing locations.

Bears are not an issue, since LBL is not part of their natural territory. Therefore, food and other "smellables" do not have to be hung or stored in a bear vault.

For more information see tinyurl.com/LBLrules.

Land Between the Lakes:
9. Canal Loop

An easy loop with views of Barkley Lake to the east, Kentucky Lake to the west, and the canal to the north.

Trail Length: 11 miles
Suggested Time: 2 days / 1 night
Map: US Forest Service: tinyurl.com/CanalLoop

Overview: The Canal Loop Trail is a good option for those wanting to backpack the LBL area without committing to the North/South Trail. The Canal Loop starts and ends at the North Welcome Station and can be hiked in either direction. But it may be better to choose your camping site preference first and then select your access point along the loop trail. There are also several connector trails shown on the on-line map which gives you even more options.

The loop alternates between ridgetop and shoreline views of both lakes and the canal. Free backpacking permits are required, as discussed on the previous page. However, a $7 backcountry permit is required if you want to camp at the Nickell Branch Backcountry Area. The Canal Loop Trail is also open to cyclists and may get crazy on race weekends. The only water available along the trail is what you can draw from the lake, unless spring rains have fallen recently. But the watershed is small and most creeks remain dry throughout the year.

Directions: To reach the North Welcome Station, take exit 31 from I-24, just east of Paducah. Head south on KY 453 for 6 miles, passing through the small town of Grand Rivers. KY 453 is also known as the Woodland Trace National Scenic Byway, or simply "The Trace." You can pick up your permit at the Welcome Station or after hours at the self-serve kiosk. Overnight parking is available here, too.

Staging: The Twin Lakes Backcountry Area is located just south of the North Welcome Station. The full-service Hillman Ferry Campground is another 1.4 miles south of the Welcome Station, just off KY 453. For more information see tinyurl.com/HillmanFerry. Other campgrounds are available in the park.

Route Description: The best camping places along the Canal Loop Trail are either on the east side along Lake Barkley, between the trailhead and the Nickell Branch Backcountry Area, or on the Kentucky Lake side of the loop just north of Connector D. If you like sunrises, you might choose to camp on the east side of the loop. But avoid the Nickell Branch area on weekends unless you want to hear the Kentucky ballgame blasting from your neighbor's radio or the sound of generators serenading the crickets and tree frogs.

Camping along the Kentucky Lake side of the loop gives you beautiful sunsets, lapping waves against rocky beaches, excellent water access, and plenty of driftwood for campfires. The western side of the loop is also more rugged than the east, with steeper ascents

Land Between the Lakes

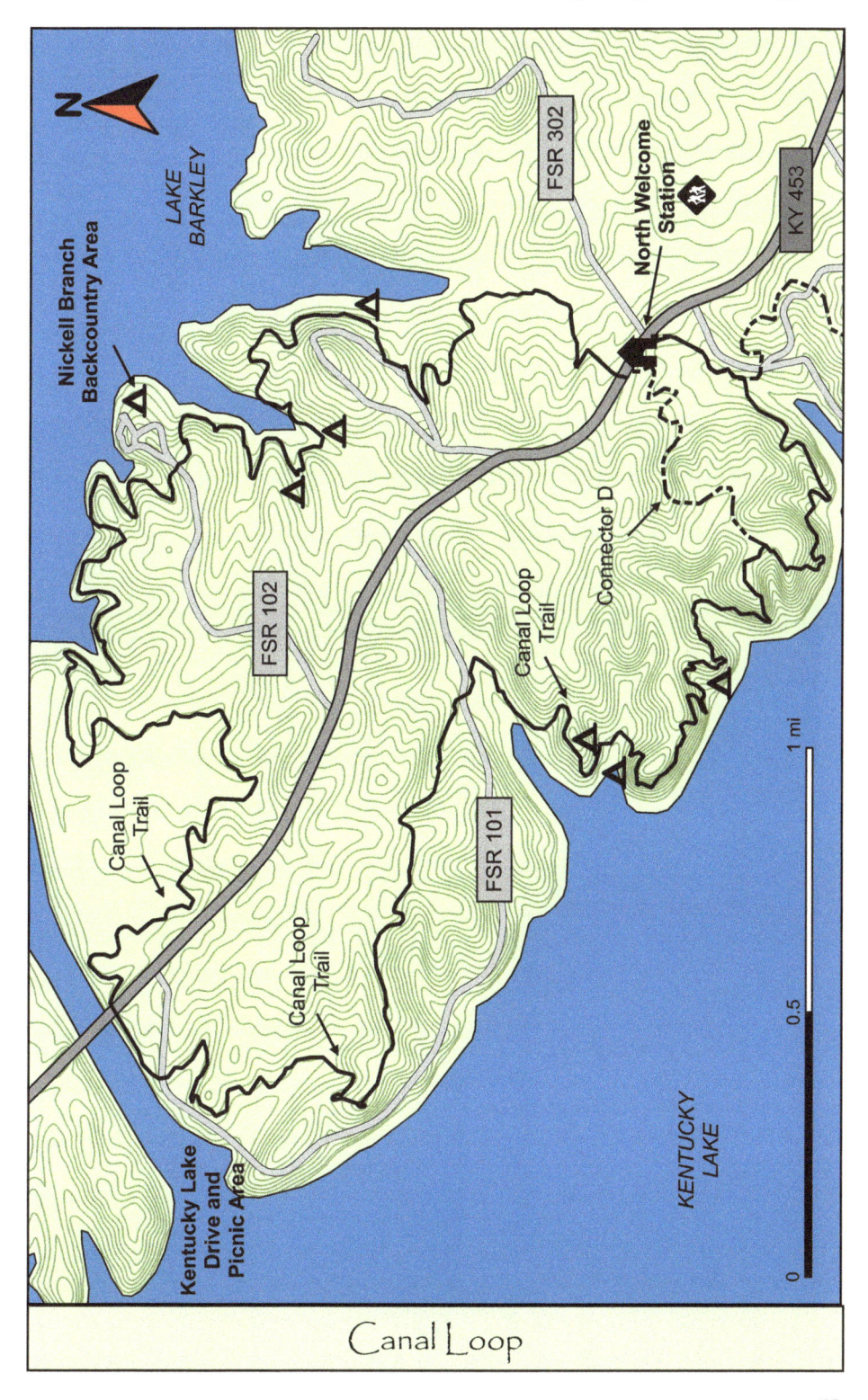

Canal Loop

53

Backpacking Kentucky

Let's begin at the North Welcome Station and take the Canal Loop Trail counterclockwise. Again, you may want to adjust this depending on your camping preferences. To pick up the trail, head northeast from the parking lot and cross KY 453. You'll see the white diamond blaze for the trail and another rogue trail on your right. Stay straight here for the Canal Loop Trail. After a mile of hiking, the trail briefly joins a gravel road near some power lines, before ducking back into the woods. A small, well-used campsite is located on the edge of Barkley Lake with good views of the water.

Hiking another 0.8 miles past this first campsite you'll find two more campsites near a wood footbridge. Neither campsite has immediate lake access, but the woodland views are rather pretty. Across the bridge a connector trail joins on your left, but bear right and hike another .75 miles to Nickell Branch. At the gravel road (FSR 102), turn right to get to the campground. The Nickell Branch Backcountry Area is 2.6 miles from the North Welcome Station.

From Nickell Branch, it's 3.2 miles before the Canal Loop Trail passes under KY 453 and the bridge over the canal. After the trail goes inland, the vista to the north resembles a savanna. A lively imagination could easily envision giraffes stretching their long necks reaching for the leaves on lower tree branches. Clearly, the river formed a delta here long ago.

Beaver girdling is common at LBL.

Under the canal bridge is your best chance at seeing a boat, even a barge, passing between the two lakes. The trail then crosses Kentucky Lake Drive (FSR 101) and heads for higher ground. Although a few of the ascents on the western side of the loop trail are somewhat steep, rarely do they climb for more than 100 vertical feet. Just past the radio tower, the trail begins a long descent along "Tower Hill" (so-named by the cyclists). There is a marginal campsite located at the mouth of the first large inlet (not marked on the map), which is only available at low water levels.

By now you have probably seen a huge selection of flotsam and jetsam along the low-lying areas near the lake's edge. Heavy rains in the summer of 2016 resulted in significant flooding, which mother nature is still rebounding from. Two other campsites (marked on the accompanying map) have good access to a nice rocky beach in a small sheltered cove.

From here the trail ascends "Money Maker Hill," with your last good camping spot near the water's edge on your right. From here it's less than 2.0 miles back to the North Welcome Station and the trailhead.

Side Trips: If you have time, be sure to check out the town of Grand Rivers. Small eateries, antique shops, full-service restaurants, and marinas dot the area. For more ideas, see www.grandrivers.org.

Land Between the Lakes:
10. North/South Trail—North End

A relatively easy trail, passing through deciduous forests, with lots of great lake views.

Trail Length: 31 miles (one-way); can be combined with the south section for 58 miles
Suggested Time: 3 to 5 days
Map: US Forest Service: tinyurl.com/LBLTrails (the Hunt Area Maps have good detail)

Overview: The North/South Trail—North End runs 31 miles from the North Welcome Station to the Golden Pond Visitor Center. Most of the trail runs through hardwood forest, with intermittent views of Kentucky Lake. There are seven springs located along the north end, although dry conditions can make these unreliable, and with easy lake access, most are not worth considering. There are also two backcountry shelters, both of which are basically quonset huts for hobbits. You really don't want to stay in these, unless you have hairy feet...

You can hike the trail in either direction, although hiking north to south might be best. However, if you're looking to hike both the North End and the South End trails consecutively, it's best to start at the South Welcome Station and hike the entire trail south to north. The South End is not as scenic and water access is more of a challenge—that leaves the prettier North End and its iconic water views for last.

It's also good if you can set up shuttle in advance and leave a vehicle parked at the opposite end. If you want to shorten the trip, the trail is also accessed by several forest service roads off KY 453.

Directions: To reach the North Welcome Station, take exit 31 from I-24 (just east of Paducah). Head south on KY 453 for 6 miles. KY 453 is also known as the Woodland Trace National Scenic Byway, or colloquially as "The Trace." To get to the Golden Pond Visitor Center from the North Welcome Station, stay south on KY 453 for another 18 miles. Just after you cross under US 68, the Visitor Center will be on your left.

Shuttle: Apparently, Land Between the Lakes does not have much of a hitch-hiking culture. So to run shuttle you'll have to bring two vehicles or contact a local business to set up arrangements. Wood-N-Wave, a bike and watersport shop owned by Jackie and Ranee, will run shuttle for you at the going rate of $2 per shuttle mile. Their motto is *Life is Short - Play Hard*. You pass the shop off KY 453 in Grand Rivers. Call (270) 362-2453 or email info@woodnwave.com. Their web address is woodnwave.com.

Staging: The full-service Hillman Ferry Campground is 1.4 miles south of the North Welcome Station, just off KY 453. For more information see tinyurl.com/HillmanFerry.

Camping: Only official backcountry camping areas are marked on the accompanying maps. There are so many "backpacking" campsites scattered throughout LBL, they are too numerous to note on the maps. You can camp almost everywhere.

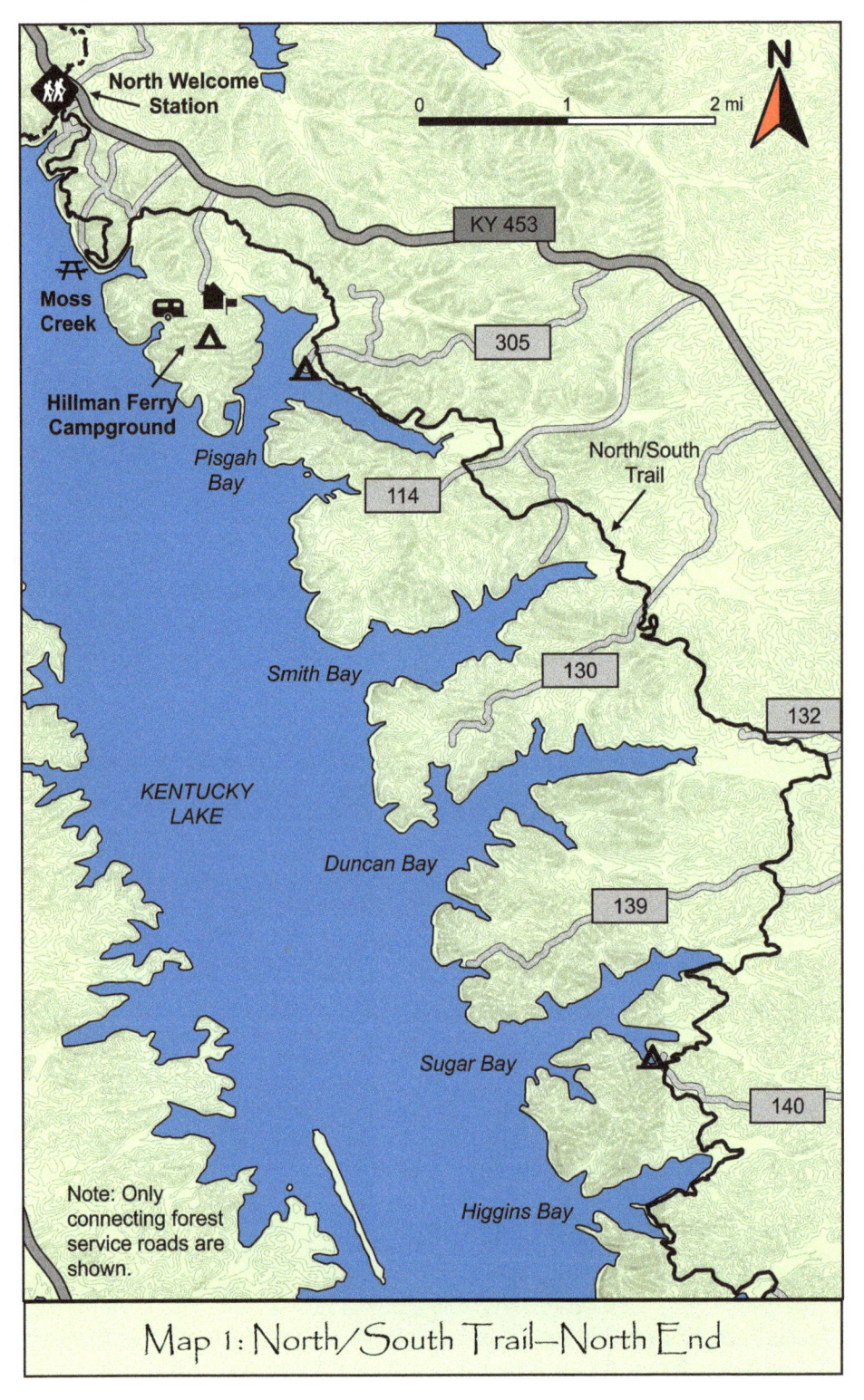

Backpacking Kentucky

Map 1: North/South Trail—North End

Land Between the Lakes

Route Description: If you're hiking the North/South Trail—North End from north to south, begin at the North Welcome Station. Follow the paved walk south of the backpacking permit kiosk. The walkway parallels KY 453 for about 100 yards before crossing a paved access road. Turn right (south) to stay on the North/South Trail. (The paved walkway runs all the way to the Hillman Ferry Campground.) In about 0.25 miles, the North/South Trail bears left and the Canal Loop Trail bears right, over a small wood bridge. Stay left. Soon the trail crosses a gravel road, FSR 104, and a mile later another gravel road, FSR 106.

Slightly over 3.0 miles from the TH, the trail descends to the Moss Creek Picnic Area. The views are gorgeous, but unfortunately it is a day-use area only. Apparently camping was permitted here years ago, but it became way too much of a party site.

Moss Creek Picnic Area.

The North/South Trail leaves from the far southern edge of the Moss Creek parking lot, passes a spur trail to Brown Spring, and then crosses the paved road (FSR 110) leading to the Hillman Ferry Campground. Don't be misled by all the places in LBL that are named "Ferry" in the park, as that's quite a misnomer and is only reflective of an era long before the rivers were dammed.

The trail continues inland until it crosses yet another gravel road (FSR 305), which leads to the Pisgah Point Backcountry Area. As a reminder, you'll need a "Backcountry Camping Permit" to camp at Pisgah. But there are several "backpacking" sites just south of here, right on the lake, with no chance of generators running all night.

From Pisgah Bay, the trail heads inland again, crossing several gravel roads, including FSR 114, 130, and 132. If you're into old cemeteries, there are quite a few to check out along this section of the North/South Trail, testimony to the early settlers who lived and died here.

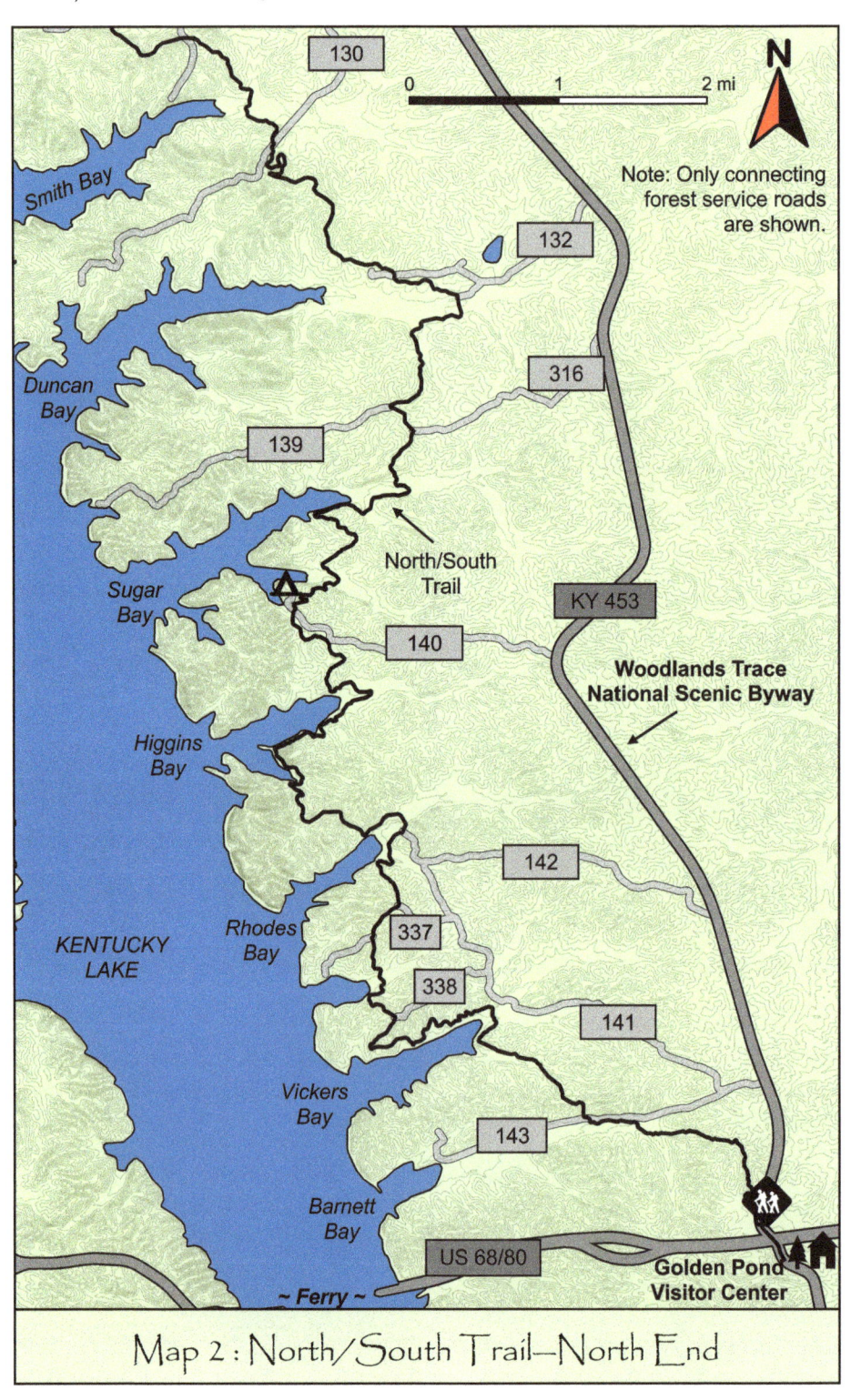

Backpacking Kentucky

Map 2: North/South Trail—North End

Look alive where the trail joins FSR 139. Bear left (east) on the gravel road for about 0.6 miles. Then bear right (south) on yet another gravel road, signed for the Pinnegar Cemetery and blazed with a white diamond. (The "Cemetery Access Only" sign refers to vehicular traffic.) In the summer of 2016, heavy rains washed out a bridge further down the trail and the Forest Service re-routed this section of the trail. The detour takes you quite a bit out of the way and if you don't mind crossing a small (typically, dry) creek, then head towards the Pinnegar Cemetery. Just before you reach the family graveyard, the trail leaves the road and bears left toward Sugar Bay.

Sugar Bay is the home of another Backcountry Area, popular amongst campers and boaters in the summer, and hunters in the fall. Again, there are several good camping spots near by, freely available for backpackers. But be forewarned, Sugar Bay seems to attract more than its fair share of hooligans on weekends who like to imbibe more than necessary.

The next bay south, Higgins, is really pretty. Right where the two inlets meet, there is an old cemetery out on a peninsula, accessible only at low water. It's amazing that this family graveyard was not moved before Kentucky Lake was formed.

Multiple opportunities exist to camp along the lake.

After Higgins Bay, the North/South Trail continues its repetitive pattern of rolling through hardwood forest, crossing gravel roads, and gracing the edges of Lake Barkley. It's not unusual to see sailboats anchored in any of the bays or fisherman plying their trade for the crappie, bass and bluegill that thrive in these waters.

After Vickers Bay, the trail remains inland until it reaches KY 453, just north of the Golden Pond Visitor Center. Be careful as you follow the blazes along the western shoulder of the highway. The trail then ducks under the US 68 overpass, before crossing the road to the Visitor Center. You may need to wash-up before using the porcelain thrones, but it's nice not to have to filter your water again.

Backpacking Kentucky

Land Between the Lakes:
11. North/South Trail—South End

An easy to moderate trail through hardwood forests, alternating between old double-track roads and some single-track pathways.

Trail Length: 27 miles (one-way); can be combined with the north section for 58 miles
Suggested Time: 3 to 4 days
Map: US Forest Service: tinyurl.com/LBLTrails (the Hunt Area Maps have good detail)

Overview: The North/South Trail—South End runs 27 miles from the South Welcome Station to the Golden Pond Visitor Center. Important differences exist between the North End and the South End of the North/South Trail. The entire South End trail lies inland, depriving hikers of the gorgeous lake views found along the North End. Equestrian riders are also permitted on 11 miles of the South End trail, although cyclists are not. Finally, water availability is more limited along the South End and more remains of "civilization" can be seen, as compared with the North End. All this doesn't mean that the South End is not worth pursuing, but backpackers should take these factors into account.

If you plan on only hiking the South End, it really doesn't matter which direction you hike the trail. But if you plan on hiking the South and North Ends consecutively, you should start south and hike north.

Directions: To reach the Golden Pond Visitor Center, take exit 31 from I-24 (just east of Paducah). Head south on KY 453 for 24 miles. KY 453 is also known as the Woodland Trace National Scenic Byway, or colloquially as "The Trace." To get to the South Welcome Station, stay south on KY 453 for another 22.3 miles.

Staging: The full-service Hillman Ferry Campground is 1.4 miles south of the North Welcome Station, just off KY 453. For more information see tinyurl.com/HillmanFerry.

Shuttle: It's good if you can set up shuttle in advance and leave a vehicle parked at the opposite end. If you want to shorten the trip, the trail is also accessed by several forest service roads off KY 453. Please read the North End description for shuttle ideas.

Route Description: There are so many "backpacking" campsites scattered throughout LBL, they are too numerous to note on the maps. You can camp almost everywhere. More importantly, you may want to stash water along the trail, particularly in the fall.

If you start from the South Welcome Station, head east on the Fort Henry North/South Trail Connector (which begins northwest of the Welcome Station). In about 1.6 miles, bear right on the North/South trail. From here the trail passes under a canopy of deciduous hardwoods, before coming to the Morgan Cemetery, located on a small spur off FSR 221. Follow the spur north, then turn right (east) onto FSR 221. In just a short distance, the trail leaves the road and bears north once again. You are about 7.9 miles from the south TH.

Land Between the Lakes

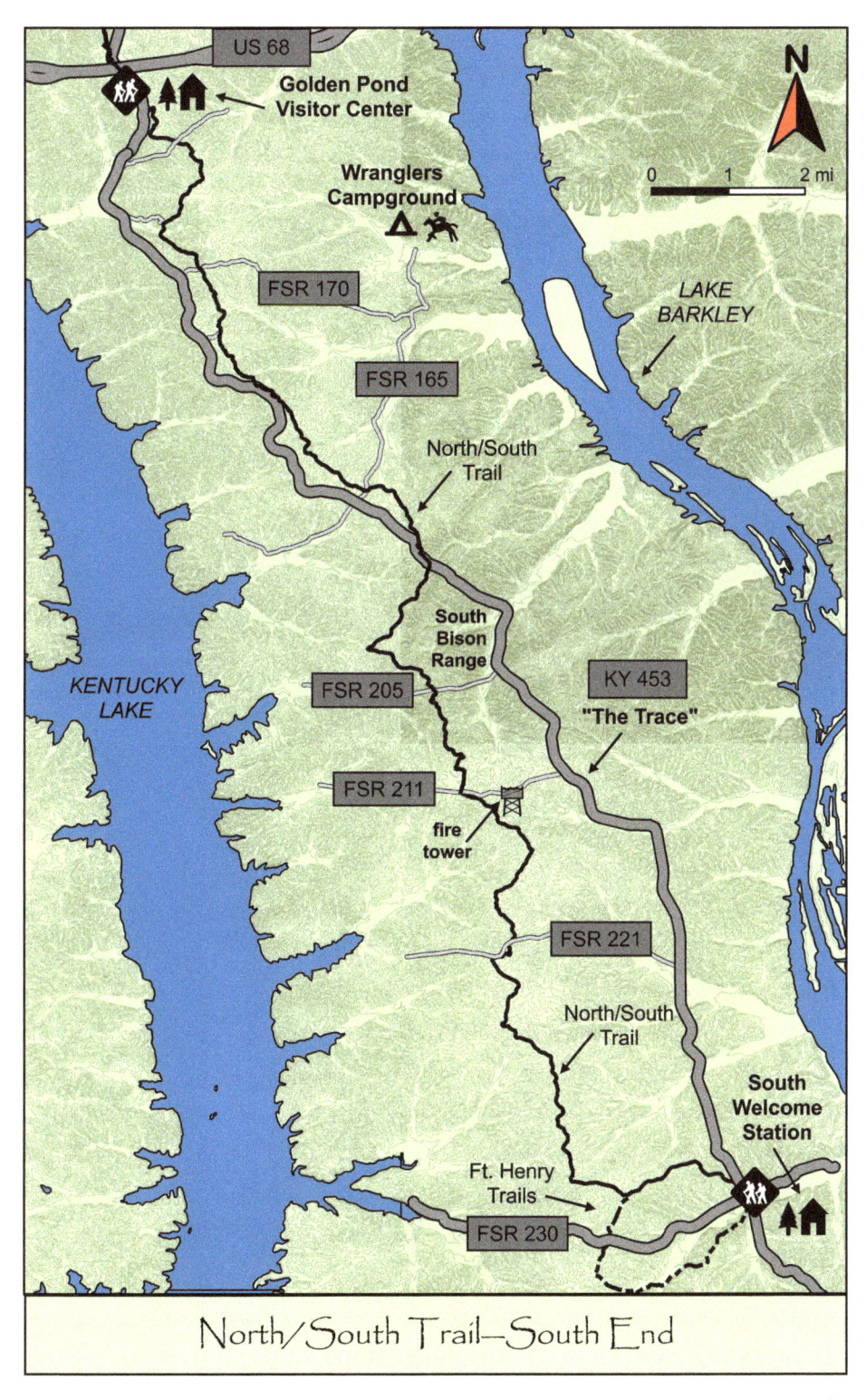

North/South Trail—South End

61

Backpacking Kentucky

Again, the trail meanders through more hardwoods, passing the Fuqua Cemetery. Just south of FSR 211, you will see a large fire tower east of the trail, which is worth checking out. From here, the trail crosses FSR 211, passes under more hardwoods, and then crosses FSR 205. If you're hiking during any of the hunting seasons, be sure to wear your neon orange. Despite strict regulations admonishing hunters that they must stay clear of any trails and roads, most hunters use these pathways as their transportation corridors.

Even Bear is decked out in his hunter-orange super cape.

If you're so inclined, you can follow FSR 205 until you reach the western side of the South Bison Range. You can follow this trail before hooking back up with the North/South Trail just before it intersects with KY 453.

Carefully cross the highway KY 453, following the North/South Trail on the eastern side of the road. Again, if you love old cemeteries, this is the trail for you. Next on the agenda is the Rushing Family Cemetery, followed by the Blossey and Bullock cemeteries. All that lies between you and the Golden Pond Visitor Center are the Remenschneider, Turkey Creek, Compton, and Ross cemeteries. But be forewarned, the trails from here to south of the Golden Pond Visitor Center get lots of horse traffic and unfortunately, the trails show it.

There are two shelters in the vicinity of the South End Trail—The Iron Mountain Shelter and the Laura Furnace Shelter. Both shelters are mini-quonset huts with fire rings. Really. You might prefer just finding your own backpacking site.

For the best maps, print out the Hunter Maps noted above. They have an incredible amount of detail, including topo lines, back roads, and scenic points of interest.

Mammoth Cave National Park:
12. Sal Hollow to Turnhole Bend
13. Bluffs Loop
14. Big Kahuna Loop

Beautiful scenery for those willing to brave the muddy quagmires.

Trail Length: 10 to 31.4 miles
Suggested Time: 2 to 4 days
Map: Mammoth Cave National Park: tinyurl.com/MCNPTrails

Overview: Mammoth Cave National Park (MCNP), touting the largest known cave system in the world, covers 52,830 acres of hardwood forest—over double that of the Red River Gorge. However, the karst topography and soil structure found in the region has rendered MCNP trails extremely vulnerable to both erosion and compaction, creating huge mud pits along many of the trails. Furthermore, the National Park Service has not written nor enforced regulations to adequately protect their multi-use trails. As a result, overuse of MCNP trails by horses and their riders have virtually destroyed many of the trails. But the park is working to improve the trail system and is in the process of updating their long-term trail maintenance and reconstruction plans. With careful timing and trail consideration, backpackers can still find a way to enjoy this special area.

Directions: Heading south on I-65 from Elizabethtown, KY take exit #53. Driving north on I-65 from Bowling Green, take exit #48. Follow KY 70 and KY 255 to the MCNP Visitor Center, about 15 minutes west of the interstate. You'll pass by more Kentucky kitsch than you can wave a rebel flag at.

Regulations: All backcountry camping must be in permitted sites. Although free, permits must be picked up in person from the Visitor Center and no reservations are accepted. Each backcountry campsite is permitted for one party, up to eight people, and two tents. No food storage requirements are in place, although hanging poles are available at each site. Water (be sure to treat first) is available nearby. Dogs are permitted on leash.

Staging: Only one full-service campground is located in the park, Mammoth Cave Campground. Maple Springs Campground has seven sites—three are group sites and four are equestrian sites. The Houchin Ferry Campground is more "primitive," but there is no ferry service to the trailheads. However, it is easy to drive around to the north side of the park. MCNP also has rustic cabins for rent.

Route Description: Many of the trails at MCNP are a real mess. In essence, your tax dollar is allowing private commercial horse stables and their customers unfettered use of this natural resource. And any economist can tell you that when goods are free, people overconsume. Think free beer at a frat party.

Backpacking Kentucky

Make no mistake…horses are beautiful creatures and many in the riding community are great stewards of the land. But at MCNP horseback riders can ride any day of the year, rain or shine, no permit required. Most park and national forest managers have already realized the permanent damage horses and their riders can do to wet soils, creek crossings, and fragile ecosystems. In many other parks, riders must buy permits to help pay for trail reconstruction and/or trail riding is forbidden in the wet spring months. The MCNP does none of this! Fortunately, the park is seriously reconsidering their polices and we hope for the best. So don't give up on MCNP yet. Let's think this through a little more carefully.

1. All of the commercial facilities catering to the horse crowd are in the north end of the park. Most riders access the trail system at either First Creek Trailhead or Lincoln Trailhead. That means Wet Prong, Blair Spring, Raymer Hollow, and parts of Mill Branch can be a disaster.

2. Head south. Few horses (and their riders) have the stamina to make it all the way down to Sal Hollow and McCoy Hollow trails. These trails also have some of the best rock formations, waterfalls, and wildflowers. However, be forewarned! All of these trails have mud pits—it's just a degree of how many and how deep.

3. Because of the karst topography, natural springs pop up everywhere, yet some creeks run dry. For example, Dry Prong of Buffalo Creek is nearly always dry. But Dry Prong Trail has a spring-fed creek running down the middle of it, rendering it one of the worst trails in the park. The irony escapes no one.

Wet Prong Creek.

4. MCNP also has several old lightly-graveled roads that are really great to hike. These roads generally run along ridges and, for the most part, are well-drained. The horses use them a lot, but the damage is limited. That makes many sections of Buffalo Creek, Turnhole Bend, and Collie Ridge trails some of the better hiking choices.

5. The heavy clay content of many Kentucky soils means that water is slow to drain. Fall or winter backpacking may be a good strategy.

6. Be flexible! With permits given out on a first-come, first-served basis, be sure to have several back-up options in mind in case the backcountry campsite you want is already taken.

Mammoth Cave National Park

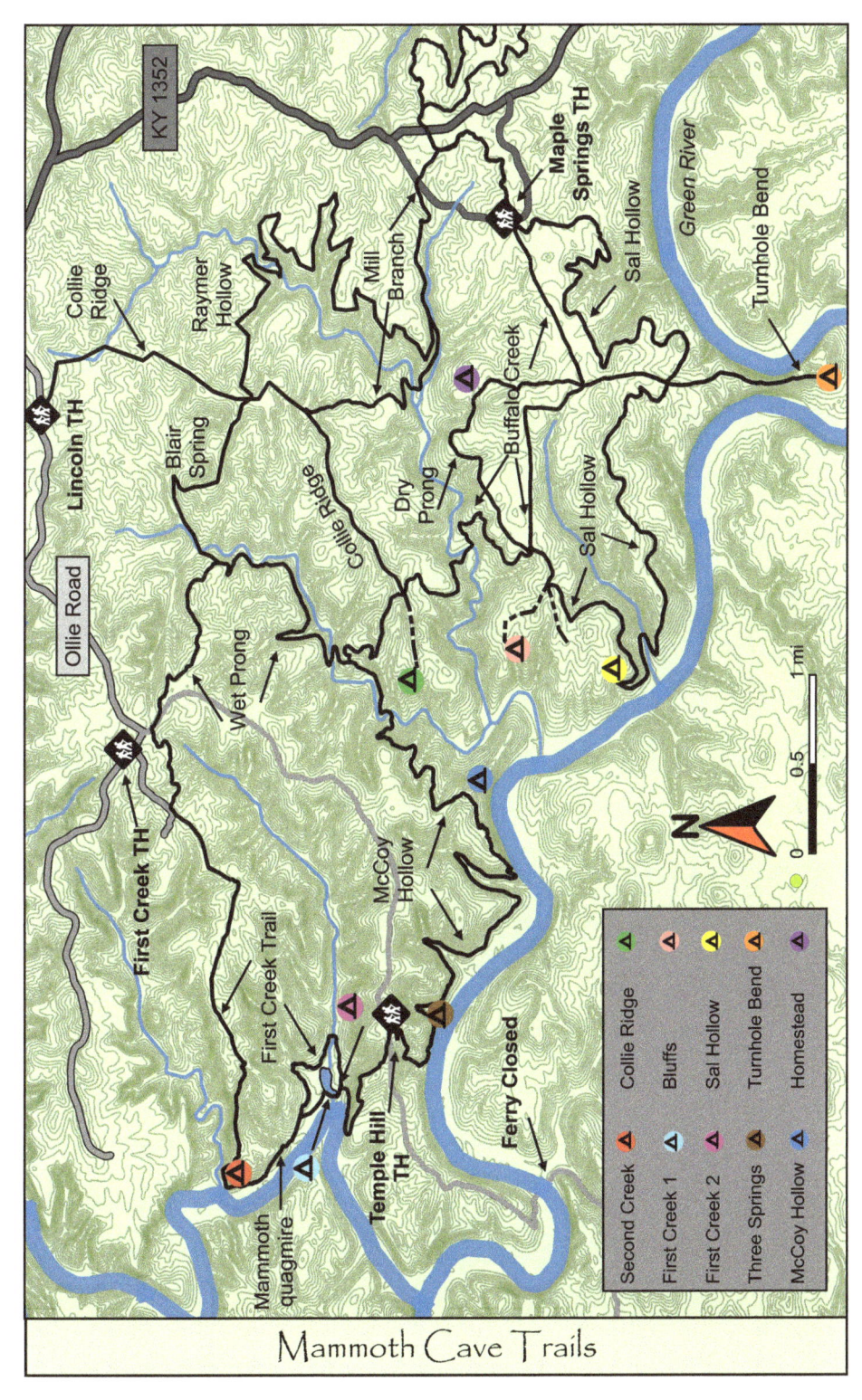

Mammoth Cave Trails

65

Possible Itineraries:

Sal Hollow to Turnhole Bend: 10 miles round-trip
Start at Maple Springs Trailhead. Follow the Sal Hollow Trail 3.8 miles to the Turnhole Bend Trail. Turn left, heading south. Hike 1.2 miles to the Turnhole Bend Campsite, which has a beautiful view of the Green River Valley. Retrace your steps the next day.

Bluffs Loop: 12.9 miles
Start at Maple Springs Trailhead. Follow the Sal Hollow Trail to the Sal Hollow Campsite, for a total of 7.2 miles. The next day, finish the Sal Hollow Trail and return along the Buffalo Creek Trail. Add the Miles-Davis Cemetery and Bluffs Trail spurs. Return hike is 5.7 miles.

Big Kahuna Loop: 31.4 miles
Only recommended when conditions are dry.

Day 1: Start at First Creek Trailhead. Follow the Wet Prong Trail to the Collie Ridge Campsite. Total 5.3 miles. Look for the waterfall spur at the end.

Day 2: Come back out on the Collie Ridge Campsite Trail. Turn right on the Buffalo Creek Trail. Another right on the Turnhole Bend Trail. Right on the Sal Hollow Trail. Camp at Bluffs Campsite. Total 9.6 miles.

Day 3: Come out from Bluffs. Turn left on Sal Hollow. Another left on Buffalo Creek Trail. Continue on Wet Prong until you get to McCoy. Turn left on McCoy Hollow. Camp at Three Springs. Total 9.4 miles.

Day 4: Continue on McCoy Hollow (one of the prettiest trails in the park). Cross the gravel road at Temple Hill, bearing left to find the trail again. Circle around First Creek Lake. Survive the mammoth quagmire. Take First Creek Trail back to your original trailhead. Total 7.1 miles.

Bluffs backcountry campsite.

Mammoth Cave National Park

Water falling from rockhouse, seen along trail to Bluffs campsite.

Side Trip: Write to the superintendent of MCNP and let them know your thoughts about the trail system. Politely demand that we work harder to protect this great natural resource, both below and above the ground.

> Superintendent
> Mammoth Cave National Park
> 1 Mammoth Cave Parkway or P.O. Box 7
> Mammoth Cave, KY 42259
> (270) 758–2183

Copy the Director of the National Park Service, 1849 C Street NW, Washington, DC 20240. Also post a note to Friends of MCNP on their Facebook page. Thanks.

Pine Mountain State Scenic Trail

The Pine Mountain State Scenic Trail (PMSST) is an incredible work-in-progress and one of the most exciting things to happen to backpacking in Kentucky in a very long time. Eventually the trail will run over 100 miles from Breaks Interstate Park to Cumberland Gap National Historic Park. Currently, 46 miles of consecutive trail is open, including the Birch Knob Section (29.6 miles) and the Highland Section (16 miles). In addition, the Little Shepherd Trail, a 38-mile multi-use trail, connects with the western end of the PMSST. You can hike each of these sections individually or join them together to form one long backpacking adventure.

Pine Mountain spans about 124 miles from Elkhorn City, KY to Jellico, TN. The sharp ridgetop, known as the Pine Mountain Thrust, was formed when the continents of Laurentia (North America) and Gondwana (West Africa) collided. The erosion-resistant sandstone, pocked with quartz pebbles, and softer limestone worked in tandem to form the overhanging rock faces or escarpment found on the Kentucky side of the mountain. For the most part, Pine Mountain has remained pristine and serves as an important travel corridor for black bear, habitat for the local deer and elk population, and protection for many endangered plants such as frostweed, rose pogonia, and yellow wild indigo.

Who owns the mountain? Everyone and no one. Taken verbatim from their web site "The Pine Mountain Trail is merely a complex arrangement of agreements, easements, understanding, even handshake agreements to allow a foot-trail across properties owned and administered by others, both private and public, across eight counties in two states." (www.pinemountaintrail.com) This trail is an amazing testimony of what vision, cooperation, and perseverance can accomplish. Simple thanks is not enough.

The Pine Mountain Trail also serves as a vital link in the new Great Eastern Trail (GET). When complete, the GET will run 1,800 miles and pass through nine states from New York to Alabama. Cooperation between these two trail associations has given the PMSST organizers access to world-class trail development knowledge and shelter construction, and provided uniform blazing. If you're interested in this ambitious project, you can read more at www.greateasterntrail.net.

If you want to hike both the Highland and the Birch Knob sections consecutively, you should start at the western Highland TH (off US 119) and finish at the eastern Birch Knob TH (off US 80, near Elkhorn City). Both trails are blazed in awesome neon lime and side trails (particularly water trails) are blazed in blue.

Regulations: No permits are required and the rules are pretty simple. There are three shelters (with privies) and one developed campsite (Jack Sautter), each available on a first-come, first-served basis. All sites have a fire ring and bear pole—otherwise you need to hang your food or use a bear vault. Backcountry camping is allowed, but to minimize impact, try to camp in a previously-used site. No motorized vehicles, biking or horseback riding is permitted between US 23 and US 119. Dogs are allowed, but technically should be on leash. Please note that dogs are not permitted in the Bad Branch Falls State Nature Preserve.

Pine Mountain State Scenic Trail: 15. Birch Knob Section

Possibly the most difficult, and most spectacularly beautiful, backpacking trail in Kentucky.

Trail Length: 29.6 miles; can be combined with the Highland Section for 46+ miles
Suggested Time: 3-4 days / 2-3 nights
Maps: PMSST: tinyurl.com/BirchKnobSection. This is a great map!
US Forest Service: tinyurl.com/PMSST-Topo

Overview: The Birch Knob Section of the PMSST is a demanding ridgetop trail, with breath-taking views both literally and figuratively. It's a tough call, but many backpackers would claim this section to be slightly more difficult and perhaps even more beautiful than the Highland Section. Challenges along the Birch Knob Section include finding reliable water sources, navigating steep ascents and descents on rock-strewn paths, and occasionally trying to figure out which way the dang trail goes.

But this sawtooth trail has the amazing ability to bring the beauty of Pine Mountain alive. Demanding climbs lead hikers to gorgeous views of distant mountains on both the Kentucky and the Virginia sides of the trail. Equally abrupt descents lead to gaps along the ridgetop, where early settlers lived off the land and mule teams carried supplies from one valley to another.

Hardwood trees dominate the wide-open canopy, while hells of rhododendron and pockets of mountain laurel thrive in the ravines and atop the ridges. Evidence of the great upthrust is found along the trail, culminating in scenic overlooks, hogbacks, and craggy rock formations. Starting at the Pound Gap, VA trailhead and finishing up in Elkhorn City results in a net loss in elevation.

Rhododendrons abloom over Kentucky. (B. Askren)

Directions: While this trail can be hiked as an out-and-back, it's best enjoyed after setting up a shuttle. It's about 27 miles (40 minutes) between the two trailheads (one-way).

To the eastern TH from Elkhorn City: At the intersection of US 80 and KY 197, follow US 80 (Patty Loveless Drive) east for 0.4 miles. Immediately before you cross the bridge over the Russell Fork River, turn right (south) on the unmarked Carson Island Road. On the right-hand corner will be City Hall, including the fire and police departments, and a sign for the Blue Hole Pay Lake. Carefully follow this gravel road for 0.7 miles, until you reach the trailhead parking lot and picnic shelter. However, locals claim that it's not the best idea to leave a vehicle at the TH. You may be better off driving back to City Hall and asking them if it's OK to leave a vehicle in their parking lot. They have a vested interest in saying "yes."

To get to the western TH in Pound Gap, VA from Elkhorn City: Follow US 80 back to Elkhorn City. Turn left on KY 197 (West Russell Street). Drive 17.2 miles. Make another left on KY 805. Drive 7 miles. Turn right on US 23/119 South. Go 1.5 miles. Bear left on US 23 South. Drive the final 1.3 miles up the mountain to the Marathon gas station on your right. Politely talk to the management and ask if you can leave a vehicle here. They will direct you where to park. Be sure to buy something from the station—maybe one more chocolate bar or a tank of gas. To find the trailhead, carefully cross US 23, bearing south towards the Valero gas station on the opposite side of the highway. Head up the paved side road to the old mountain café, which is now Mountain Life Church. The TH is just before the church.

Staging: If you want to get an early start on the trail, Breaks Interstate Park is 7.3 miles southeast of Elkhorn City. Carr Creek State Park is located just outside of Whitesburg.

Route Description: As noted previously, you may want to start at the Pound Gap TH to take advantage of the overall loss in elevation as you hike towards Elkhorn City. With nearly 30 miles of hiking ahead of you (more with all the spurs to various points of interest and water sources), you'll want to plan your trip carefully. The following route assumes that you will spend three days on the trail. The proposed itinerary gives you time to run shuttle the morning of day one.

Day 1: Pound Gap TH to 4 Springs—7.2 miles (Map 1)

Once you pass the radio tower near the TH, the trail quickly becomes scenic, beginning with the views at Raven's Nest. Just past the rock overlook, descend the stone steps to two small caves on your right. Beyond this is the Skyview Rockhouse (or rockshelter), which you absolutely don't want to miss. It's down a short spur to your right and well worth the time.

About 4 miles from the TH you'll descend to a small clearing in the woods at Bryant Gap. An old metal farm gate will be on your left and a logging road continues straight ahead. Bear right (heading northeast) and hike down another old logging road. Near the bottom of this hill, and just beyond a large stack of poplar logs on your left, will be another clearing. Bear left (at 10 o'clock) and head up another old road. The blazes on the trees here occasionally disappear, but you should be fine.

In another 1.5 miles you will come to the quarry overlook on the Kentucky side of Pine Mountain. It's obvious that resource extraction is the backbone of the economy here, but gratefully you see little of this on the Virginia side. Shortly after you pass the quarry,

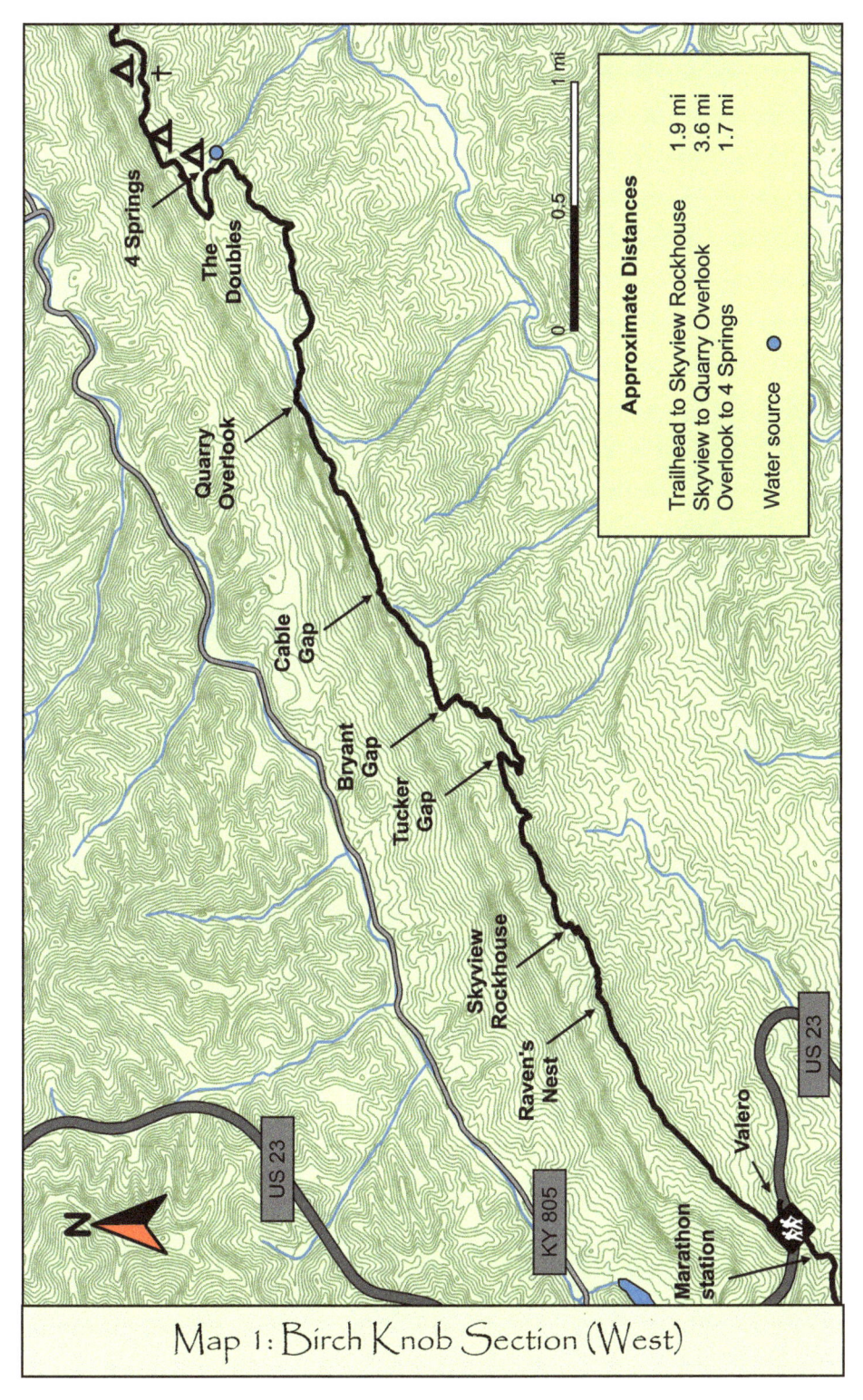

Pine Mountain State Scenic Trail

Approximate Distances

Trailhead to Skyview Rockhouse	1.9 mi
Skyview to Quarry Overlook	3.6 mi
Overlook to 4 Springs	1.7 mi

● Water source

Map 1: Birch Knob Section (West)

Backpacking Kentucky

Bears aren't the only ones who use this trail as a transportation corridor.

part of the original Birch Knob section has been rerouted south of the twin knobs known as "The Doubles." This re-route adds a little bit of mileage from what is shown on the official trail map.

Your first campsite will be at 4 Springs, part of which is a bog in early spring and a flat as summer approaches. But there is plenty of dry ground here and reliable water year-round. After a prolonged dry spell the springs may slow to a trickle, but you can always dig a small hole in the creek bed and wait for it to fill before collecting your water. If this campsite is taken or not satisfactory in any way, you can hike a bit further to another campsite along the trail.

Pine Mountain State Scenic Trail

Day 2: 4 Springs to Birch Knob Shelter—8.6 miles (Map2)

After leaving no trace at 4 Springs and hiking about 0.75 miles, you'll pass a small cemetery on your right, holding the remains of John Cable and a few other early settlers. Just past the cemetery, the trail crosses a gas line right-of-way. An old home site and the foundation of a springhouse will be on your left at Osborn Gap. This area has a nice large campsite, but no reliable water source is close by.

The next large campsite and water source is at Cantrell Gap. What's the big deal about water up here? Remember the discussion of the formation of the escarpment and hogbacks along the ridgetop of Pine Mountain? Any rainfall that arrives or natural spring water tricking forth, quickly runs down the steep mountain hillsides. Consequently, the PMSST traverses a very small area of the mountain's watershed, rendering water a valuable resource.

Grassy Gap features another steep descent in the trail and some interesting rock formations. While settlers cleared rocks for use in building foundations, rock fences, and boundary lines, these rock formations appear to be small abutments, used for perhaps protecting the gap with rifle fire.

Another 0.6 miles past Grassy Gap, the PMSST joins the gravel road leading to the Birch Knob Observation Tower. Bear left on the road and walk 0.1 miles to find the small spur trail leading to the picturesque Mullins Pond. Go ahead and pull some water here if you need to, because the next source is another 2.6 miles from here.

The next 2.5 miles of hiking may quickly become your least favorite as the trail follows a gravel road 1.0 mile up, 0.5 miles down, and a final 1.0 mile up to the Birch Knob Observation Tower. The road is really not that bad, but on beautiful weekends the locals drive up here for the beautiful views and think anyone walking this mountain road must be crazy. Maybe we (happily) are.

Morning light over Virginia.

Backpacking Kentucky

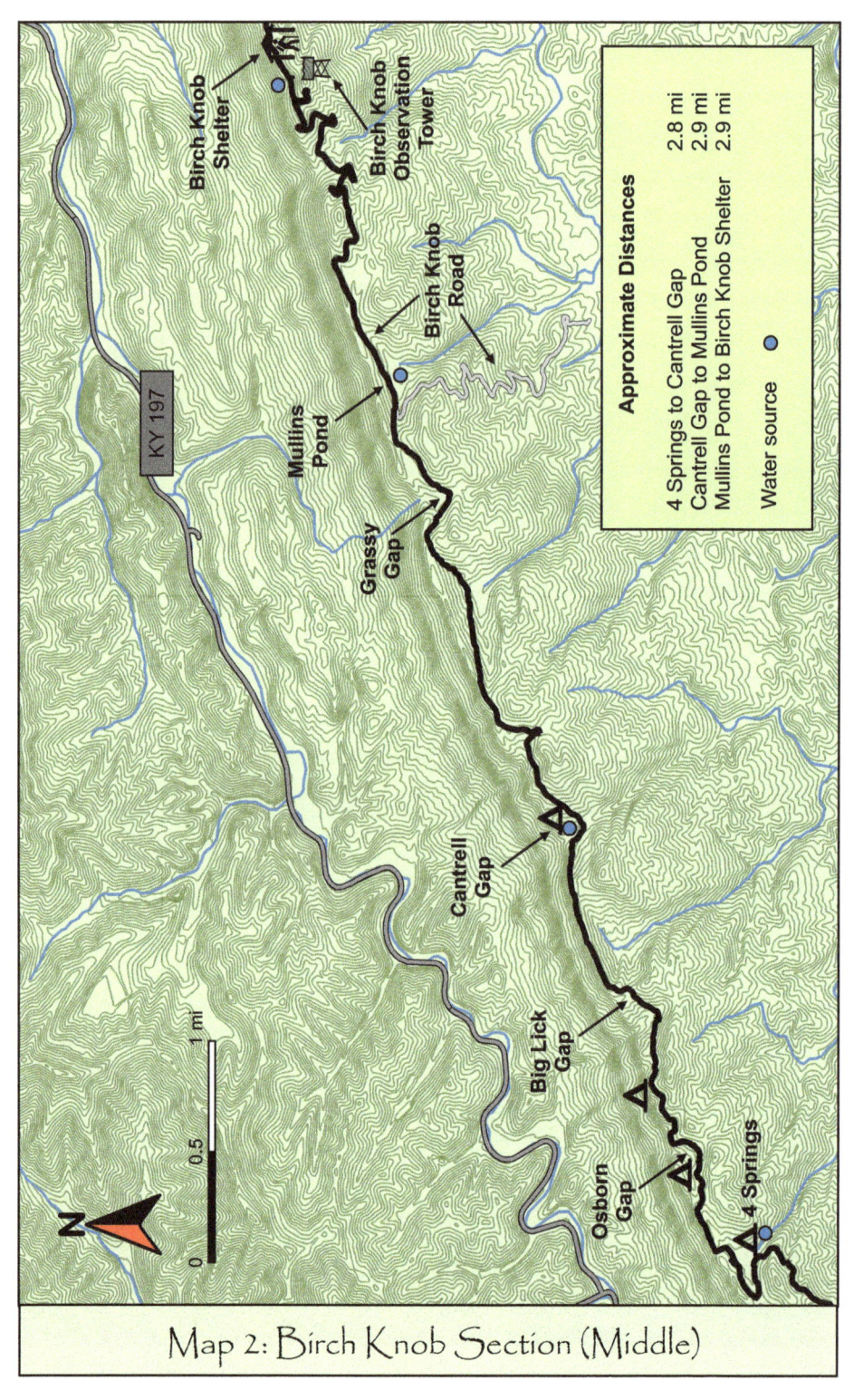

Map 2: Birch Knob Section (Middle)

Approximate Distances

4 Springs to Cantrell Gap — 2.8 mi
Cantrell Gap to Mullins Pond — 2.9 mi
Mullins Pond to Birch Knob Shelter — 2.9 mi

Water source ●

Pine Mountain State Scenic Trail

Autumn dusk at the Birch Knob Observation Tower.

    The Birch Knob Observation Tower replaced the wood fire tower that stood here, keeping watch from the highest elevation point along Pine Mountain, standing at 3,273 feet above sea level. Follow the short spur road to the base of the tower and climb the 184 steps leading to the observation deck and the spectacular 360-degree views awaiting you. And if you can manage sunrise or sunset visits, be sure to come back again.

    After leaving the observation tower, continue along the trail until you see a small cistern and two pipes extending beyond. This water is some of the best you'll find along the trail, but be sure to treat it first. It's a short 0.2 miles to the Birch Knob Shelter from here.

    The shelter is an excellent place to hang up your pack, put up your feet, and enjoy the quiet of the woods. In addition to a large fire pit, the shelter also offers a bear pole for hanging food and a clean, self-composting privy. Be sure to check out the hiker's journal and add a few notes of your own. While there is water available along the trail to Jenny Falls, it may be easier to return to the cistern to be re-supplied.

Birch Knob Shelter.

Backpacking Kentucky

Map 3: Birch Knob Section (East)

Approximate Distances

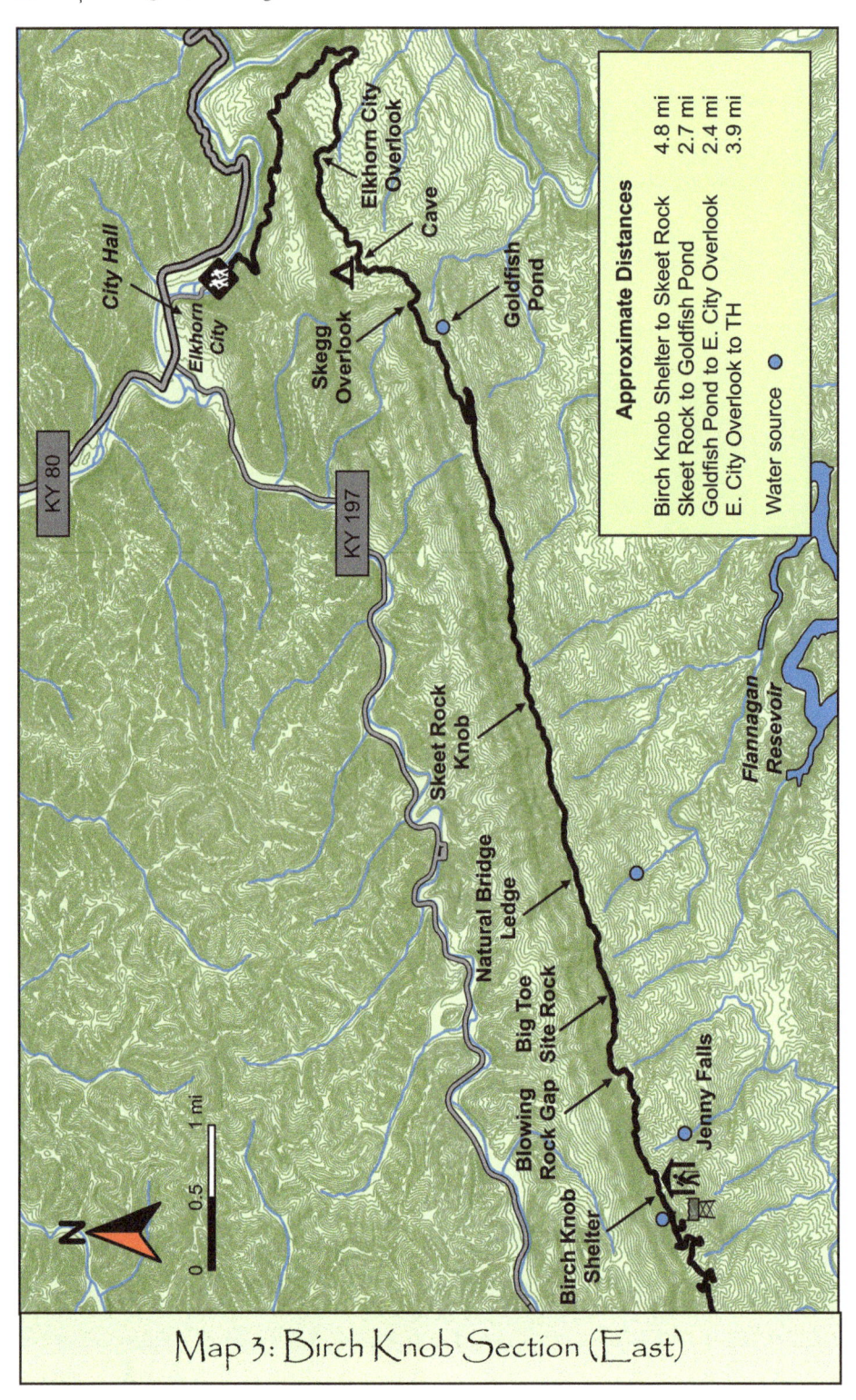

Birch Knob Shelter to Skeet Rock	4.8 mi
Skeet Rock to Goldfish Pond	2.7 mi
Goldfish Pond to E. City Overlook	2.4 mi
E. City Overlook to TH	3.9 mi

● Water source

Day 3: Birch Knob Shelter to Elkhorn City TH—13.8 miles (Map 3)

You'll want to get an early start if you expect to make the Elkhorn City TH before dark. Water availability and good camping are in short supply along this final section of trail, so plan accordingly. Plus, you'll want to take extra time to relish the sights.

From the Birch Knob Shelter it's only 1.5 miles to the gorgeous views starting at Big Toe Site Rock. Again, you'll have to look past the resource extraction on the Kentucky side of the mountain. But the overlooks and rock formations are stunning.

Before you get to Natural Bridge Ledge, there are two water trails leading to an old homestead with a cistern. But the hike requires quite a scramble down the hillside and may not be worth the effort. Otherwise your next reliable water source is Goldfish Pond.

While the sights and sounds of the humongous electrical tower and power lines perched atop Pine Mountain overwhelm the view at Skeet Rock Knob, the sights along the trail before and after the knob are dazzling. The overthrust and hogbacks are clearly evident along this 2.0 miles of trail.

The PMSST then descends from the ridgetop and follows an old dirt road, before doubling back upon itself. Follow the road about a mile until you reach Goldfish Pond. If you have a charcoal filter be sure to use it to freshen the taste of the water. Continue along the road, passing an old cemetery on your left, until you get to Skegg Overlook. Shortly thereafter, the trail ducks back into the woods (on your right) and heads up an extremely steep hillside. Right after "The Cave," which might prove hard to find, is a very nice, large campsite and a small creek that may have water available in the spring and early summer.

Your last big view is at the Elkhorn City Overlook. From here, the trail originally descended about 2.2 miles before reaching the eastern TH. But recent trail realignments have extended this last section to almost 4.0 long, long miles. Follow the road down to the TH and park shelter. Maybe have someone drop a pack and hoof it back to City Hall to grab your vehicle. This will give you time to consider donating time and/or money to the Pine Mountain Trail Conference. They have given you so much.

Sunset view from the Birch Knob Observation Tower.

Pine Mountain State Scenic Trail:
16. Highland Section

A challenging trail with spectacular views and gorgeous scenery.

Trail Length: 16 miles; 18.2 miles, including the spur to Bad Branch Falls. Can be combined with the Highland Section for 46+ miles.
Suggested Time: 3 days / 2 nights
Maps: PMSST: tinyurl.com/HighlandSection. This is a great map, too!
US Forest Service: tinyurl.com/PMSST-Topo

Overview: The Highland Section of the Pine Mountain Trail runs from just outside Whitesburg, KY to the Kentucky/Virginia state line south of Jenkins, KY. The trail stays mostly ridgetop along Pine Mountain and offers outstanding views, strenuous climbs and descents between knobs and gaps, and a close-up look at the beautiful ecosystem of southeastern Kentucky. Spring hikers are rewarded with an outstanding wildflower show, including one of the highest densities of pink lady slippers and flame azaleas in Kentucky. Early summer brings a bounty of blueberries free for the picking, while fall promises vistas of blazing autumnal colors. The only time you might want to avoid this trail is mid-to-late summer when water sources run low and the humidity runs high. Snowy and icy conditions should also be avoided due to multiple rock scrambles along the trail.

Directions: While this trail can be hiked as an out-and-back, it's best enjoyed after setting up a shuttle. Distance between trailheads is about 16.6 miles (22 minutes).

To the western TH: From Whitesburg, KY where KY 15 Ts into US 119, follow US 119 west for 4.7 miles. On your right you'll see a large sign for The Little Shepherd Trail. Take an immediate right on KY 1679 and another right into the large gravel lot. You can leave a vehicle at the far end of the parking area. The Little Shepherd Trail starts here and goes in the opposite direction (west) of the Highland Trail. It's hard to see, but on the other (eastern) side of KY 119 is a small wooden staircase leading up into the trees. That's where the Highland Section trail starts.

To the eastern TH: From Whitesburg, KY where KY 15 Ts into US 119, follow US 119 east for 10.3 miles. Turn right on US 23, heading towards Pound, VA. Drive about a mile up the mountain to Pound Gap. There is a Marathon gas station on your right. Politely talk to the management and ask if you can leave a vehicle here. They will direct you where to park. Be sure to be a good store patron. To find the trailhead, face the dumpsters at the far back of the Marathon parking area. There is a large undeveloped rocky lot to your right. Look carefully and you'll see the trailhead at the far back corner of this lot.

Staging: If you want to get an early start on the trail, Carr Creek State Park and campground is located just outside of Whitesburg. There is also a shelter and a developed campsite on each end of the Highland section, just a short distance from either trailhead.

Pine Mountain State Scenic Trail

Route Description: For the most part, the Highland Section trail is amazingly well blazed and signed. But before we begin, a note about mileage…the official map shows the Highland Section at 14.7 miles. The trailhead sign says it's more and several backpackers have recorded higher mileages in the 17-18 mile range. But what are a few more miles on a trail this beautiful?

The Highland Section can be hiked in either direction. The western trailhead, off US 119, starts at about 2700 feet elevation. The eastern trailhead off US 23 at Pound Gap, stands at about 2450 feet elevation. So traveling west to east you have a small loss in elevation, but truthfully there is so much up and down on this trail, it's not enough to notice. But the route described below assumes you'll hike west to east, so let's get going. After crossing US 119, take the wooden stairs and follow the trail up through the forested area. Once you reach the gravel road, turn left. You'll quickly come to an intersection of more gravel roads. Look across this junction and just to the right you'll see a blaze where the trail ducks back into the woods.

Bear sighting at the Flamingo Shelter. (B. Askren)

The Flamingo Shelter is located just 0.4 miles from the trailhead. The shelter is really nice, quite large with two sleeping platforms, picnic table, bear pole, privy, and fire ring. There are also several flat spots for tent camping. Occasionally people hike in just for an overnight and aren't always the tidiest campers, but thoughtful trail angels tend to pick up the slack. If you need water, there is a small stream just down the trail past the shelter, although water levels can be meager later in the year. Even if you don't spend the night, it's fun to read the journal kept in the large plastic tub.

Leaving Flamingo Shelter, about 0.3 miles of hiking brings you to the sign-in box. Be sure to add your details before climbing the stairs. Eagle Arch is just another tenth of a mile, down a small slope on your left. The section between Eagle Arch and Lemon Squeezer is a really pretty one. But be forewarned, if your load is too wide, the juice will run. Not marked on the map is a small creek just past Lemon Squeezer with water available pretty much year-round.

Backpacking Kentucky

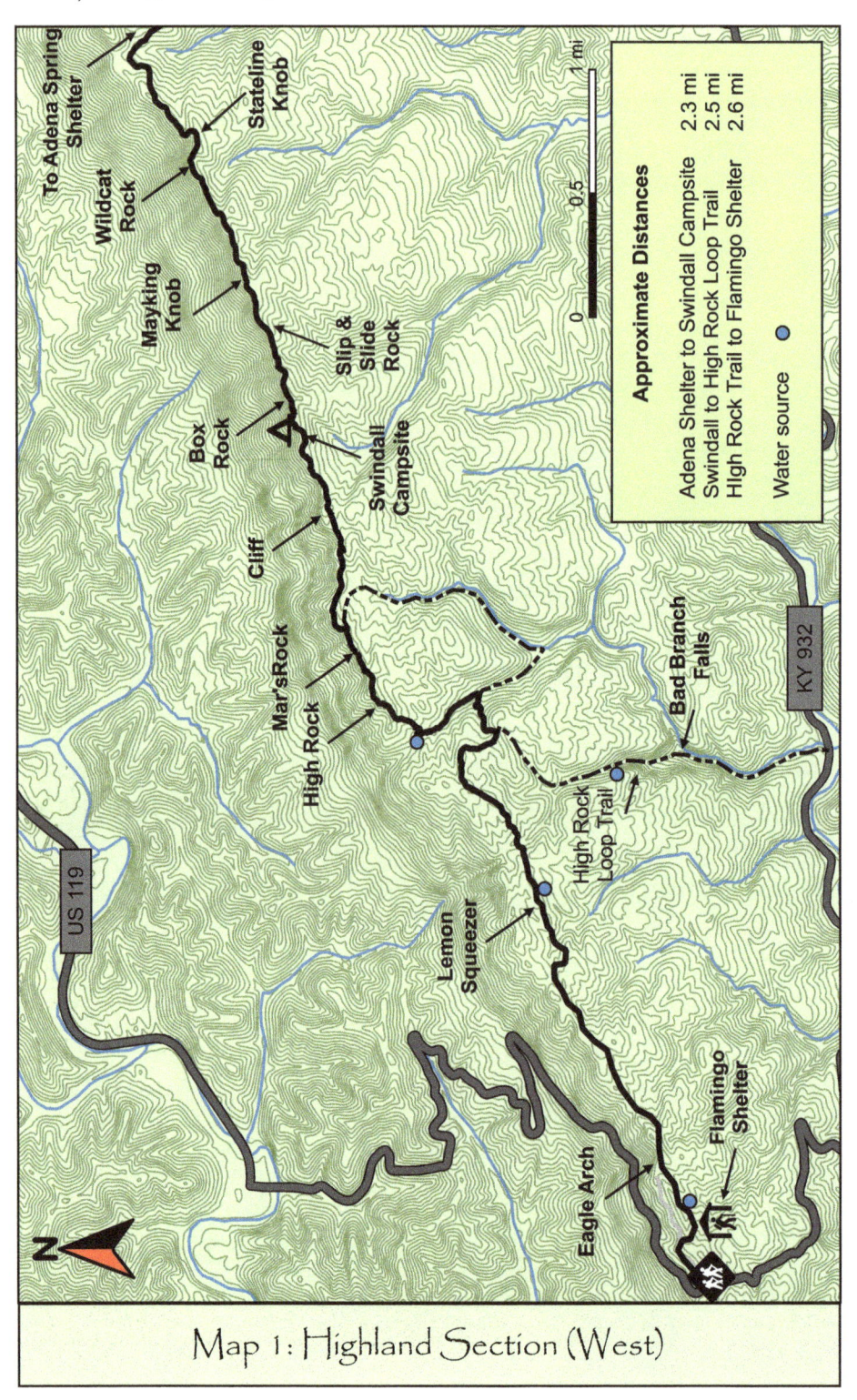

Map 1: Highland Section (West)

Pine Mountain State Scenic Trail

Less than a mile from Lemon Squeezer, the High Rock Loop Trail comes in on your right, leading to Bad Branch Falls, which lies in the Kentucky State Nature Preserve of the same name. It's a little over a mile to the falls and well worth the hike. If you do take the trail to the falls, it is blazed in red. You may be able to find a place to stash your packs to make the hike back up a little easier. It's also important to know that while dogs are permitted on the Pine Mountain Trail, they are not allowed in nature preserves. But if you have the chance, be sure to take this optional spur.

Puttin' on the squeeze at Lemon Squeezer. (B. Askren)

Back on the Highland Section trail, the High Rock Loop Trail joins the main trail for 0.2 miles, before splitting off again to your right. Keep left here, staying with the neon lime blazes, through another really sweet part of the trail. During the month of May, there are so many pink lady slippers along the Highland Section that even King Arthur's court would be pleased. Another off-map creek lies deep in the drainage, right before you make the climb to High Rock. This water has a slight sulfur odor, but is perfectly good to drink after treating.

The trail along High Rock and Mar's Rock are excellent examples of the hogbacks that dominate this mountain ridge. The trail crosses many of the hogbacks formed atop Pine Mountain years ago when the African and American continents drifted together, creating a powerful upward thrust of rock plates that covered the earth's surface. Typically the hogback itself has an equal declination on both sides, although over time the softer

Bad Branch Falls. (K. Bartell)

81

rock below has eroded while the harder rock cap on top has remained, forming an escarpment. The name hogback comes from the bumpy ridges formed atop the ridge, like a hog's back. The Arkansas Razorbacks don't have anything on Kentucky.

About halfway between Mar's Rock and Box Rock is a great rock wall, referred to as the "Cliffs" on the map. From here, the trail continues to climb to Box Rock. The campsite at Swindall is undeveloped as of this writing. There is a small open area with only one tent spot of decent size and a small fire pit. You can squeeze in another tent or two on the trail itself, although there are several good spots for hanging hammocks. There is no water available here, so plan accordingly. Despite these caveats, Swindall is a great place to savor the night with incredible sunsets over Kentucky and sunrises over Virginia. In the evening and early morning, fog settles in the valleys like cotton batting from an old quilt. Nights bring the occasional yipping of coyotes on the next ridge, which subsides as daybreak invites songbirds to herald the new day.

View from Mars Rock is outta' this world. (B. Askren)

The section from Box Rock to Stateline Knob is a series of shorter ups and downs. Slip and Slide Rock is another example of the great up-thrust and Mayking Knob is the highest point along this portion of Pine Mountain. The segment from Stateline to Adena Spring Shelter is another gorgeous section, thick with rhododendron hells and lush ferns. Shortly before you reach the shelter, there are two watering holes—one at the creek on your right and another flowing from a spring beneath a small rock house on your left. At both locations, the sweet water flows through small pipes and is some of the best water on the trail. The Adena shelter is very similar to Flamingo, except at Adena there are few, if any, flat spots for tent campers. Again, be sure to read through the journal entries and add your own thoughts.

The trail from Adena to Indian Grave Campsite is a series of more ups and downs through hardwood forest. Again, at this writing, Indian Grave is a primitive backcountry site with a few flat spots and fire pits, but no other amenities. Although water availability is marked on the official map, it is quite a scramble down a long hillside and really not worth pursuing. But the breezes are good here and you're sure to have the place to yourself.

From Indian Grave Campsite it's about 2.6 miles to Twin Cliffs Overlook, which offers good views off to the north. While you can find blueberries all along the Highland trail, there are some huge bushes here patiently awaiting you or the local bear population to indulge. Although water is marked on the official map just past the turnoff to the overlook, the drainage is really puny and difficult to get to.

Less than a mile from the overlook is a really nice developed campsite, Jack Sautter. There are two tent pads prior to reaching the campsite and two at the site. A bear pole and fire pit is available. To find the water, follow the blue blazes down the old road. Be sure not

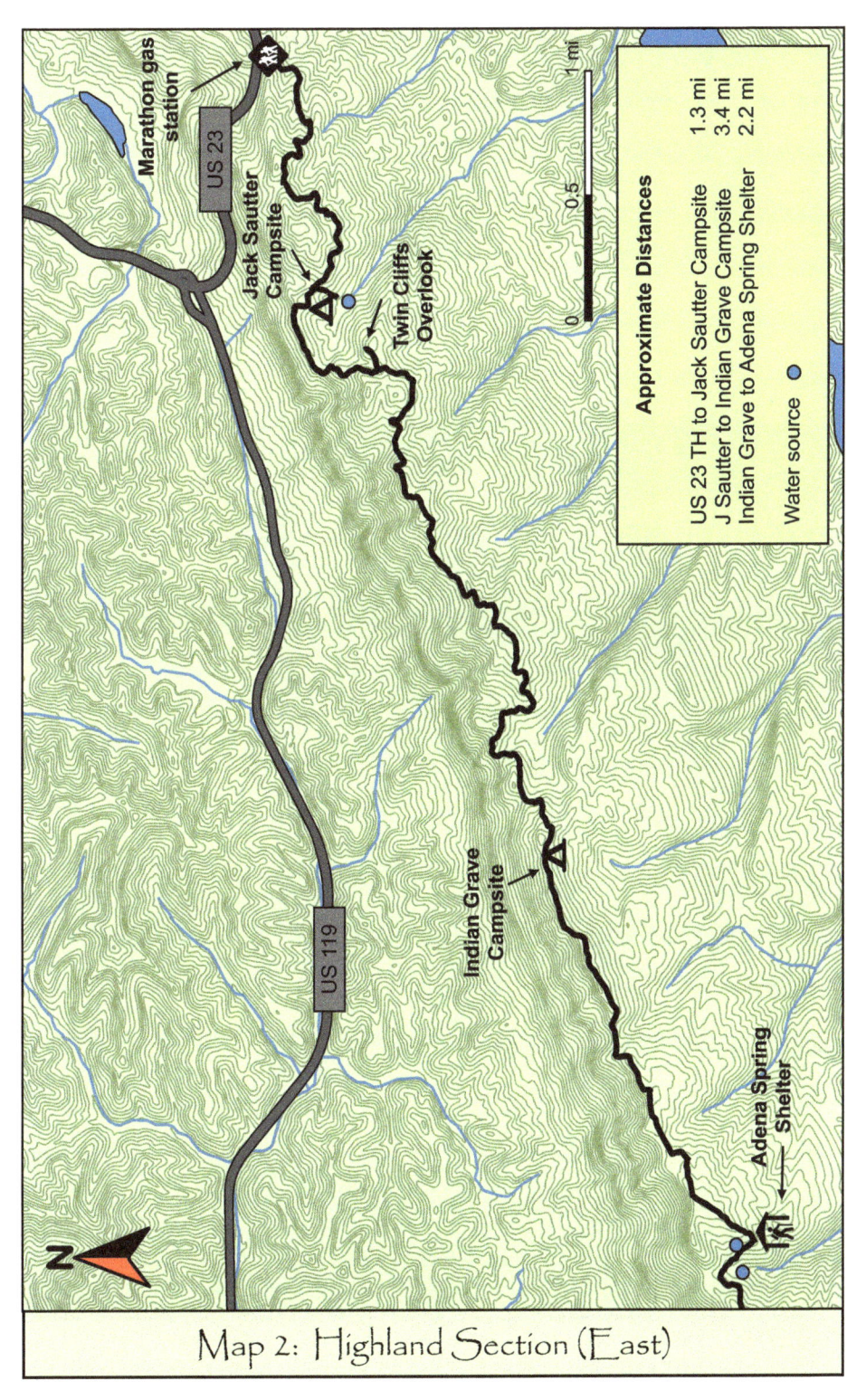

Pine Mountain State Scenic Trail

Approximate Distances

US 23 TH to Jack Sautter Campsite   1.3 mi
J Sautter to Indian Grave Campsite   3.4 mi
Indian Grave to Adena Spring Shelter   2.2 mi

● Water source

Marathon gas station

US 23

Jack Sautter Campsite

Twin Cliffs Overlook

US 119

Indian Grave Campsite

Adena Spring Shelter

Map 2: Highland Section (East)

Backpacking Kentucky

to miss the trail where the road takes a hard right. You want to stay straight to get to the creek. There are two access points down here—neither has lots of water, but hopefully it's enough.

From Jack Sautter you're only 1.3 miles to the Marathon gas station. A portion of the trail follows an old road. Just keep an eye out for the lime blazes and you should be fine. There are plans to build a new shelter close to the trailhead, down Red Fox Trail on your right. You can call it a trip once you hit the Marathon station, or cross the road and carry on to Birch Knob.

Side Trip: From the Pine Mountain Trail web site, follow the link to Join Our Efforts. Generously consider giving volunteer time, cash donation or both to the effort. It's a wonderful legacy.

Flame azaleas bloom in late spring. (B. Askren)

Watching the morning fog lift from Pine Mountain. (K. Bartell)

Pine Mountain State Scenic Trail:
17. Little Shepherd Trail

An old road that runs high along the crest of Pine Mountain.

Trail Length: 38 miles (14 miles, recommended route); can be combined with the Birch Knob and Highland sections for up to 86 miles.
Suggested Time: 4 to 6 days (2 days / 1 night, recommended route)
Maps: tinyurl.com/LittleShepTr (for a larger map tinyurl.com/LittleShep)
US Forest Service: tinyurl.com/PMSST-Topo

Overview: The Little Shepherd Trail (LST) follows KY 1679 along the crest of Pine Mountain and is a vital link between the Pine Mountain State Scenic Trail and Cumberland Gap. The multi-use "trail" varies from a one-lane paved road to a deeply rutted gravel and dirt surface. The LST is open to hikers, backpackers, equestrian riders, and motorized vehicles. A four-wheel drive vehicle is recommended if you decide to drive any portion of the trail. Although it's not quite ready for prime time backpacking, the LST is presented here as a "trail" currently under construction.

Scenic overlooks, rock outcroppings, hardwood forests, mountain laurel, and rhododendron dominate the Little Shepherd Trail. Primitive camping is permitted in Kentenia State Forest, the Jefferson Memorial Forest, and in some parts of Kingdom Come State Park (see below).

Directions: While this trail can be hiked as an out-and-back, it's best enjoyed after setting up a shuttle. If you are looking for other access points, KY 1679 also crosses KY 160 and KY 2010.

To the eastern TH: From Whitesburg, KY where KY 15 Ts into US 119, follow US 119 west for 4.7 miles. On your right you'll see a large sign for The Little Shepherd Trail. Take an immediate right on KY 1679 and another right into the large gravel lot. You can leave a vehicle at the far end of the parking area. The Little Shepherd Trail starts here and goes in the opposite direction (west) of the Highland trail.

To the western TH: From Harlan, KY drive north on US 421 for about 6 miles. At the top of the mountain, you will see the remains of Mac's Rescue Mission on your right. Turn right (east) on KY 1679. You should not leave a vehicle parked here.

Regulations: Practice Leave No Trace Principles and camp out of sight from the road.

Staging: There are five primitive camping spots at Kingdom Come State Park. They include a fire pit and hanging pole, and run $8 per night. The park service will open up additional primitive camping space, as needed. The park is in operation from April 1 through October 31.

Backpacking Kentucky

Paved portion of the Little Shepherd Trail.

Route Description: The Little Shepherd Trail offers occasional vistas of both Kentucky and Virginia on either side of the mountain ridge. While the deciduous canopy provides deep shade in the summer and colorful autumn hues in the fall, pockets of rhododendron and mountain laurel remain green all year. Rocky outcroppings, hogbacks and other interesting rock formations are found along the trail. Water is scarce up here, so be prepared. Bears are also prevalent in this part of the state, so remember to hang your food or bring a bear vault.

While the entire LST is open to backpacking, your best bet is the 14-mile section from Pound Gap (where US 119 meets KY 1679, just south of Whitesburg) to Kingdom Come State Park. The road runs through the Jefferson National Forest (which straddles the KY/VA state lines) and is open to backcountry camping.

The far western end of the LST (where US 421 meets KY 1679, just north of Harlan) is quite rugged, particularly the first few miles. Quite honestly, the local community living at the western end of the LST is not accustomed to hikers, let alone backpackers, and may not welcome you with open arms. But time and patience can go a long way in making the Little Shepherd Trail a great extension of the Pine Mountain State Scenic Trail.

One of many residences at the school.

Side Trip: If you have time, be sure to stop at the Pine Mountain Settlement School, founded in 1913 as both a boarding school for southeastern Kentucky youth and as a social center for the community. Currently, the school provides environmental education and workshops from grant writing to mushroom production, as well as programs in culture and traditional arts. For more information see pine-mountainsettlementschool.com

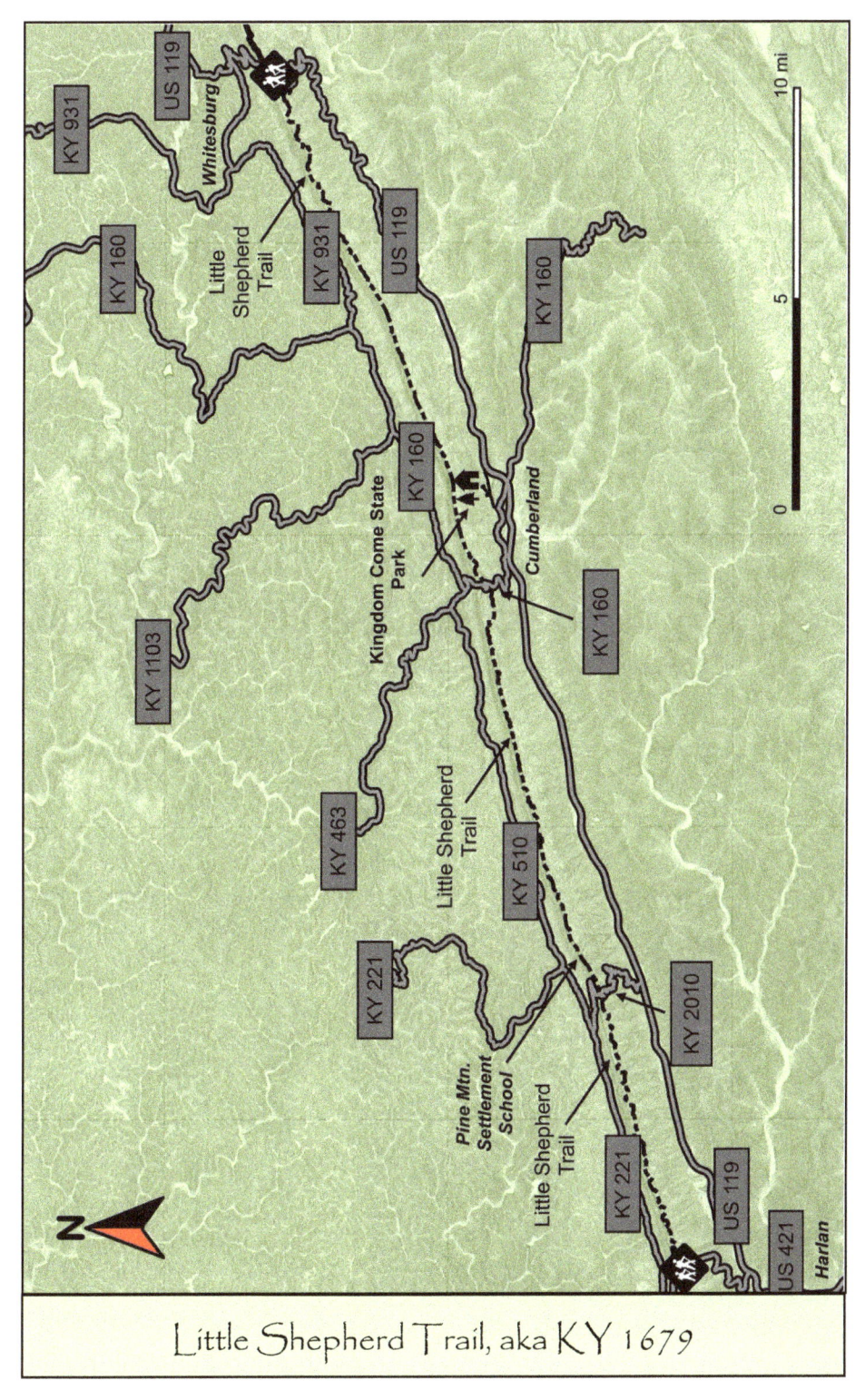

Pine Mountain State Scenic Trail

Little Shepherd Trail, aka KY 1679

Red River Gorge Geological Area

Nationally renowned for its sandstone arches and world-class rock climbing opportunities, it's hard to believe that 50 years ago the Gorge was in danger of being destroyed. Plans were made and funds were appropriated to build a dam on the Red River, which would have reduced flooding downstream, but also would have submerged one of the most spectacularly beautiful areas in Kentucky. Sometimes we get lucky when big money doesn't win out.

The Red River Gorge Geological Area is widely seen as one of the most beautiful areas in Kentucky. Clear mountain streams, towering lush hemlocks, white and pink rhododendrons, plunging and cascading waterfalls, and a plethora of fascinating rock formations attract visitors from all over.

It's difficult to piece together one large backpacking loop in the Gorge, due to its topography and trail system layout. Hikers then have the choice of running a shuttle or they can double-back on some trails to get more mileage. The proposed routes rely on the latter, but as you can see from the maps, lots of other great options exist, too. But whatever route you choose, be prepared for a roller coaster of a hike dropping down into deep drainages before climbing back up ridgetop, only to repeat the pattern all over again.

Regulations: Recreational permits are required for all backcountry camping between the hours of 10 pm and 6 am. A permit will run you $3/day (or $5/3 days, $30 for an annual pass), and can be obtained from the US Forest Service, many outfitters, and some stores (including the Shell gas station in Slade). Buying permits on-line has been a little sketchy. The permit should be displayed in your vehicle—just leave it on your dash or hang it from your rear-view mirror. Don't take it on the trail with you!

Camping is not permitted within 300 feet of any road or developed trail, nor 100 feet from the base of any cliff or the back of any rockshelter. Fires, including camp stoves, are not permitted within 100 feet from the base of any cliff or the back of any rockshelter.

All foodstuffs and garbage must be stored in a bear-resistant container or properly suspended at least ten feet clear off the ground at all points; suspended at least four feet horizontally from the supporting tree or pole; and suspended at least four feet from any other tree or pole adjacent to the supporting tree or pole (per US Forest Service regulations).

For more information on all these topics see http://1.usa.gov/1SIGVjl.

Mountain laurel in early summer.

Red River Gorge Geological Area: 18. Auxier Ridge and Double Arch

This is a great loop trail, beginning with scenic ridgetop views, before descending to the base of Courthouse Rock, then leading to an out-and-back spur to Double Arch.

Trail Length: 8.9 miles
Suggested Time: 2 days / 1 night
Maps: OutrageGIS.com
Redrivergorge.com
US Forest Service: tinyurl.com/AuxierTrails

Overview: While many view Auxier Ridge as a day hike, backpacking the area allows hikers to enjoy all the spur trails and exquisite rock formations that make this part of the Gorge special. The ridge offers spectacular views of Hay Stack Rock, Raven's Rock, Courthouse Rock, and Double Arch.

Directions: Follow the Bert T. Combs Mountain Parkway to Slade, KY exit #33. At the bottom of the ramp turn left on KY 11 towards Slade and then right on KY 15 (south). Travel 3.3 miles. Turn left on Tunnel Ridge Road and drive another 3.7 miles. Just past the wood fence, the gravel road dead-ends into the Auxier Ridge parking area.

Staging: There are several parking areas off Tunnel Ridge Road with access to easy camping. No parking is permitted along Tunnel Ridge Road itself—only in the lots. Just be sure to display your overnight parking permit and camp 300 feet away from the road or any established trail. Any of these spots make for a good staging area if you want to get an early start the next day. While pit toilets are located at the parking lots, no water is available. Be sure to bring your own water before hitting the trail!

Route Description:
Auxier Ridge Trail #204—2.1 miles
Auxier Branch Trail #203—1.0 mile
Double Arch Trail #201—0.8 miles (from junction with #203 to the arch)
  (round-trip = 1.6 miles)
Auxier Branch Trail #203—1.0 mile
Courthouse Rock Trail #202—2.4 miles
Junction of CRT/ART and back to parking lot—1.0 miles
(mileage to campsites off end of gravel road is not included)

Auxier Ridge Trail (#204) leaves from the northeast end of the gravel parking area. Again, be forewarned... there is not any water up on the ridge and your first place to fill up won't be until you reach Auxier Branch Creek. At the trailhead you will also notice a sign for Double Arch Trail, which leads directly to the arch. While this is a viable option, the trail mostly follows a gravel road (no motorized access), which makes for less than scenic hiking.

Backpacking Kentucky

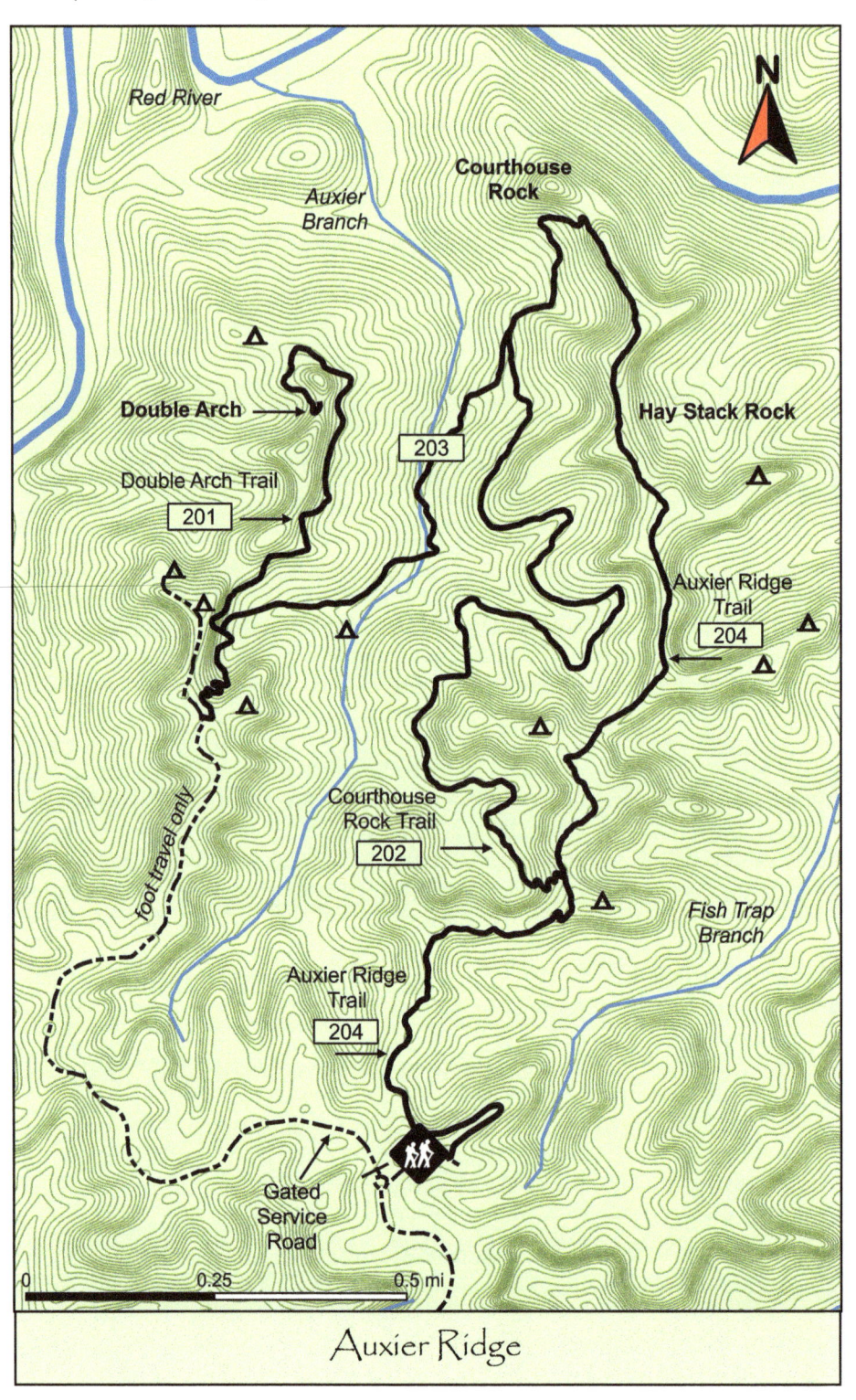

Auxier Ridge

Red River Gorge

The first section of the Auxier Ridge Trail has some good views, but fire damage and pine beetle devastation has left the area looking a bit bedraggled. But persevere, as the upcoming panoramic views of distance ridges and valleys are what make this trail so popular. Less than a mile from the trailhead, the Auxier Ridge Trail meets with the Courthouse Rock Trail. Bear right to stay ridgetop and follow the loop counterclockwise.

Courthouse Rock in the distance.

For the next mile, the trail heads due north along Auxier Ridge with spectacular views left and right, including Double Arch, Haystack Rock, and Raven's Rock. Take your time, as there are tons of great photo opportunities along this section. You will see several small spurs leading to camping sites, but only legal spots at least 300 feet from the trail have been noted on the accompanying map. Camping atop Auxier Ridge is a popular option—it's an easy hike from the parking lot, cool breezes are almost guaranteed, sunrises and sunsets can be spectacular, and stargazing phenomenal. Plus, pink lady slippers found in mid-spring and blueberries in mid-summer are always a treat. On the downside, some of the campsites can be a little untidy and the lack of water requires good planning.

At the far northern end of the ridge, the trail descends a long set of stairs before reaching the base of Courthouse Rock. This is a great place to explore, so take your time. The trail then continues back to your left, as it heads south toward the Auxier Branch Trail (#203). Bear right where Courthouse Rock Trail comes in on your left. The Auxier Branch Trail follows a small creek known as, not surprisingly, Auxier Branch. This is one of the few places you'll be able to refill water bottles.

The creek and multiple springs in the area make this part of the trail the best for spring wildflowers. Bluetts, crested iris, red and white trillium, rue anemone, phlox, May apple… and the list goes on. A keen eye may even discover showy orchis, yellow lady slippers, large-flowered bellworts, and jack-in-the-pulpits. But this trail is also delightful in

Backpacking Kentucky

the winter, as the towering hemlock, rhododendron, and mountain laurel keep a lush, green look to the landscape.

After leaving the creek, the Auxier Branch Trail begins a slow ascent up to the next ridge until it T's with #201. Turn right onto Double Arch Trail (#201). From here it is about 0.8 miles to Double Arch. Ironically, when viewed from Auxier Ridge it's actually easier to see how this arch got its name. You can also scramble or take the carved sandstone stairs to the top of the arch for more good views of Auxier Ridge, Courthouse Rock, and Haystack.

Yellow Lady Slipper *Red Trillium* *Showy Orchis*

Given that this is your halfway point, you may want to be on the lookout for a good backcountry camping spot. But given there's not any water up here, you may want to return back to the Auxier Branch Trail (by backtracking your steps along Double Arch Trail and taking a left) to camp closer to the creek. Alternately, you can continue south on Double Arch Trail until you hit the gravel road. There are a few ridgetop camping sites found close by that provide cool breezes and good views.

After backtracking on the Auxier Branch Trail, the return loop follows Courthouse Rock Trail (#202) for a little more than 2 miles. From here the trail passes under large oaks and hemlocks, before climbing out of the drainage and reaching Auxier Ridge once more. Take a right on the Auxier Ridge Trail and head south to the parking area. You have less than a mile to go before you reach your vehicle.

Side Trip: Many would argue that a trip to the Gorge would not be complete without pizza and an Ale-8-One at Miguel's, located at 1890 Natural Bridge Road, Slade, KY 40376. Miguelspizza.com. Gluten-free options are also available.

Alternately, a newer spot in the area is the Red River Rockhouse, with lots of locally-sourced options. Mouth-watering tacos (fish to pork and more), burritos, kale salad, carrot cake, and a fine selection of beer and wine makes this place worth the 5.8 mile drive from the intersection of the Mountain Parkway and KY 11 (just south of Natural Bridge State Resort Park). Located at 4000 KY 11, Campton, KY. Closed Tuesday and Wednesday. Redriverrockhouse.com. (859) 668–6656.

Red River Gorge Geological Area:
19. Heart of the Gorge

Towering hemlocks, lush rhododendrons, crystal streams, panoramic views, sandstone arches, rockshelters, plunging waterfalls, lady slippers in late spring, blueberries in midsummer, and a riot of color in fall... did we miss anything?

Trail Length: 32.1 miles (including an optional 2.4-mile spur)
Suggested Time: 4 days / 3 nights
Maps: OutrageGIS.com
Redrivergorge.com
US Forest Service: tinyurl.com/RRGorge
A free USFS topo map can be printed from http://1.usa.gov/1SXtpIp

Overview: By stringing together Swift Camp Creek and Rough Trails, the Sheltowee Trace, and sections of many other trails, backpackers can create a nice balloon or lollipop loop. This allows the adventurous hiker to see Rock Bridge, Turtle Back Arch, Angel Windows, Gray's Arch, and D. Boons Hut. An optional spur to Hanson's Point is also suggested.

All trails in the Gorge are blazed with the same white diamond, with the exception of the Sheltowee Trace, which is marked with a white turtle blaze. However, each trail junction is well signed, so saddled with a good map, you should be fine. Finally, keep in mind that water flows down hill and the creek drainages are where you'll find water. Camping is generally found along creek bottoms or up on some of the broader ridges, but there is no water access at the latter. Most of the terrain between the ridges and the creeks has a steep enough slope that camping is not feasible, unless you brought your hammock.

Directions: Follow the Bert T. Combs Mountain Parkway. Take exit #40 for Beattyville. Turn right (north) on KY 15 N. Drive 0.7 miles and then take another right on KY 715. (Sky Bridge Station will be on the right-hand corner.) In 0.4 miles you will see a gravel road on your right and a sign to the Rock Bridge Picnic Area on your left. A right-hand turn and 3 miles of driving will take you to the picnic area and trailhead.

Staging: If you are planning for a long first day, you'll want to get an early start on the trail. While there is no camping at the TH, there are several backcountry spots off Rock Bridge Road. Just keep an eye out for old logging roads or trails, and camp at least 300 feet from the road. In addition, there is no water at the TH itself—only pit toilets. There are also several developed campgrounds in the area, and the lodge or cabins at Natural Bridge State Resort Park may be a good choice for some.

Route Description: Some people like to be told where to go. Others like to wing it. And as noted above, there are a ton of different trip variations. But you may want to read the following to get an idea of what you might see along the way and some indication of expected mileage. Just don't forget to leave your permit visible in your vehicle.

Backpacking Kentucky

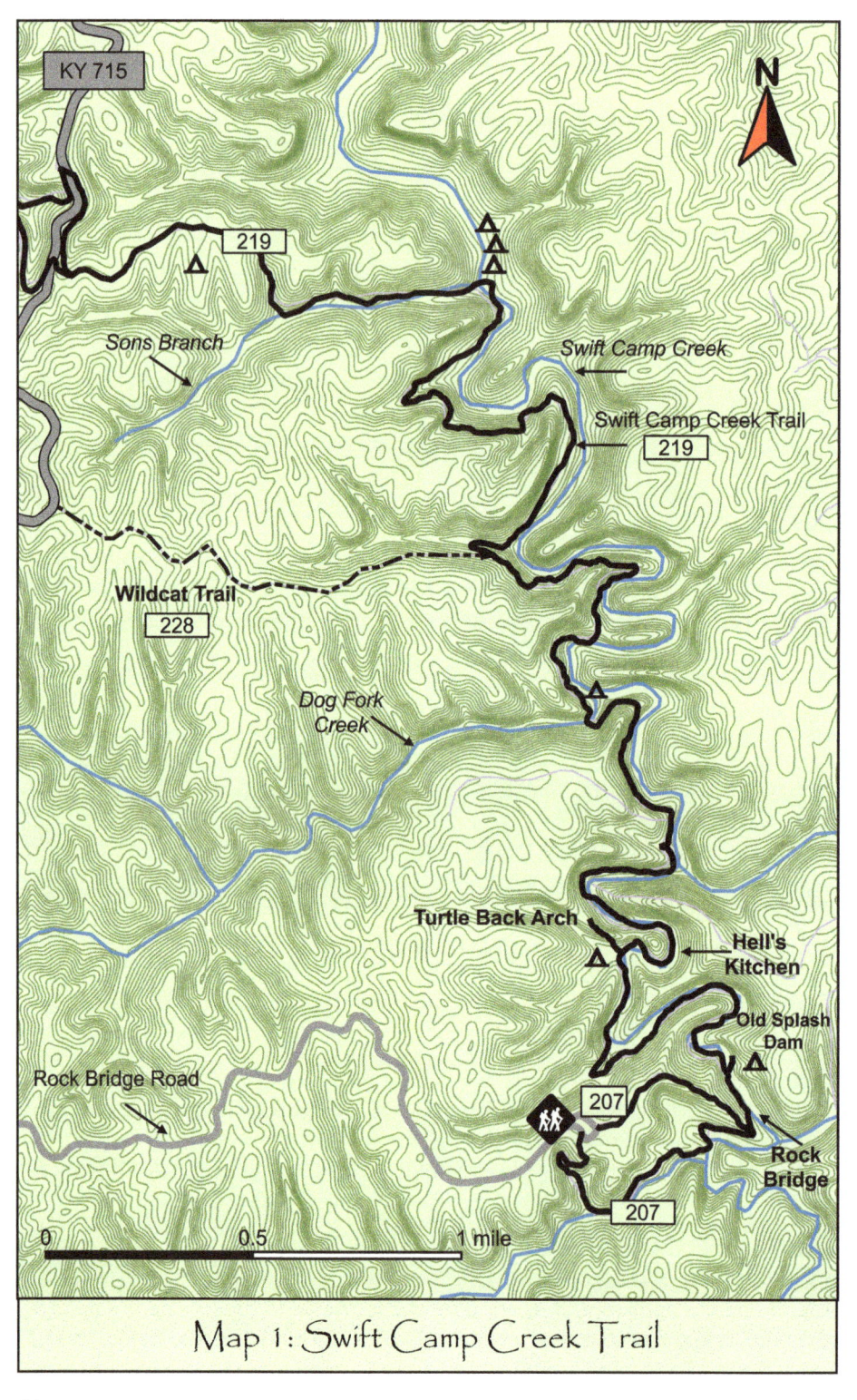

Map 1: Swift Camp Creek Trail

Red River Gorge

Day 1: Rock Bridge Picnic Area to Parched Corn Creek—8.3 miles
    Rock Bridge Trail #207—0.9 miles
    Swift Camp Creek Trail #219—6.8 miles
    Rough Trail #221—0.6 miles
    Optional Spurs to: Turtle Back Arch (0.3 miles rt), Angel's Windows (0.7 miles rt)

The trip starts at the Rock Bridge Picnic Area, within what is known as Clifty Wilderness. Technically this area is outside (but adjacent to) the Red River Gorge proper, but few people know that and even fewer care. Once at the picnic area, you can park anywhere along the gravel road or in one of the small lots. The TH you want is on the far southern side of the loop. (Not the TH starting close to the vault toilets, found on the eastern side of the picnic area.) Begin by taking the Rock Bridge Trail #207 in a counter-clockwise direction. The trail immediately descends several carved stone steps, before reaching a large rockhouse on your right at Rockbridge Fork. Bear left and continue following the trail until you see a small cascading waterfall, also on your right, known as Creation Falls. The cool spring-fed water pours over the rocks into a good-sized sandy bowl, a popular treat in summer.

    Just past the falls the trail joins Swift Camp Creek, named after the legendary John Swift who came to the Gorge in the 1760s and supposedly discovered a large silver mine. Swift ran short of money (should tell you something right there), returned to England looking for additional investors, was thrown into prison because of his left-leaning political beliefs, lost his eyesight while in the hoosegow, and died a pauper. Since then (and probably before then), no silver has ever been found in the Gorge, but some people just won't give up.

    Back on the trail, a few more minutes of walking will bring you to Rock Bridge, which traverses Swift Camp Creek. Rock Bridge is the only true "bridge" in the Gorge that spans water and one of the few in the world. Hence, Rock Bridge has graduated beyond the nomenclature of simply being an "arch." It is believed at one time the creek flowed over

Water runs clear and cool in the Gorge.

the bridge, undermining the soft limestone below the arch's sandstone cap, until the creek successfully eroded the underbelly of what is now the bridge. Indian petroglyphs use to grace the bridge, but regrettably have been erased over time.

In the late 19th century, most of the trees in this area were harvested for timber and the logs were floated down Swift Camp Creek. During that time there was a small settlement located near Rock Bridge, consisting of a gristmill, dam, and cording factory. Not many years later, a huge logjam on Swift Camp Creek broke loose, the direct result of heavy rains upstream. The subsequent flooding of water and timber destroyed the settlement, which was never rebuilt.

Local lore also has it that someone once tried to dynamite Rock Bridge, but thankfully their skill fell short of their desire, and the effort failed. Definitely a "hey guys, watch this" moment that was never uploaded to You Tube.

A little past Rock Bridge, trail #207 bears left up the hill and back to the picnic area. You will want to continue straight (north) on Swift Camp Creek Trail #219. For the next several miles the trail follows the creek downstream and ranges from easy to moderate hiking. On the map you can locate a few interesting places to explore. The old Splash Dam held freshly-cut logs before they were floated downstream, but there's really not much to see any more. Hell's Kitchen is really cool and can be accessed by walking at low water a few hundred yards downstream from the old dam.

About 1.5 miles from where you first joined Swift Camp Creek Trail, you'll see a large rockhouse nestled down a steep hillside on your right and hear the sound of Turtle Falls. It's a tough climb to get in and out of this area, so you may be content with only the views from the top or dropping your pack for a rock scramble. Then continue along #219, walking atop the rock house and crossing the small stream that feeds the falls.

If you want to see Turtle Back Arch, read this paragraph. Turtle Back Arch is an excellent example of an arch formed by two eroding rockhouses on opposing sides of a narrow ridge. While the arch is worth a visit, it's not easy to get to, particularly with a pack on your back. Just past the aforementioned stream, turn left on an unmarked trail and walk through several backcountry campsites. Bear right up the hill, then scramble up over several rock ledges and multiple rock faces, until you are up on a ridge. Continue heading northwest along the ridge until you reach the arch. It's only about 0.15 miles off the main trail, but it is a bit of a climb.

Return to the main trail and hike for about another 2.5 miles. After crossing scenic Dog Fork Creek, you'll see Wildcat Trail (#228) come in on your left. Stay straight on #219. Another 1.5 miles of hiking will bring you to Sons Branch, where Swift Camp Creek Trail makes a hard left (westerly) turn. If you're worn out, there are several good camping spots on the other side of Swift Camp Creek. The next half-mile of trail is a little strenuous, as the path begins a 300-foot vertical climb up to a nice ridge. Another mile of ridgetop hiking will give you time to decide if you want to take the 0.7-mile (round-trip) spur to Angel's Windows. There are one or two campsites atop the ridge, but no water is available.

When you are just west of KY 715, you'll see the trail split. A left at this Y will take you past the roadside sign for Angel's Windows (see Map 2). Cross KY 715 for a short out-and-back hike to a small set of arches just west of the highway. The trail continues past the arches another few hundred yards if you have the energy to explore. On the other side of the parking lot for the Angel's Windows trailhead is an old wood sign explaining "parched corn." Given this is where you're headed next, it makes for a good read.

Red River Gorge

Return back to Swift Camp Creek Trail (back on the east side of KY 715) and hike the last bit of #219. Cross KY 715 once more, where #219 joins Rough Trail #221.

Rough Trail #221 descends almost immediately, passing Frankenstein Rock on your right and Sheep Shearer's Cove on your left. Multiple rockhouses can be seen on the left side of the trail, quietly guarded by huge moss-covered boulders, majestic hemlocks, and lush ferns. A little over 0.5 miles from the road, Rough Trail crosses a pretty little stream named Parched Corn, which holds wild, but wily, brook trout.

Council Flats, downstream of the trail.

For camping, head downstream on one of the rogue trails that follow this creek. Great overnight spots can be had on both sides of the stream. The largest campsite on creek-left is known by some as Council Flats. You can take water out of the stream, but please don't put anything back into it—let's keep it pristine for the trout.

Day 2: Parched Corn to Rush Branch—6.2 miles
Rough Trail #221 – 3.25 miles
Spur to Hanson's Point – 2.4 miles
Rough Trail #221 – 0.5 miles

Continue following Rough Trail #221 upstream along Parched Corn Creek until you begin to climb back up out of the drainage. There is a magnificent rockshelter near the top of the ridge. Oh if these rocks could speak. After traversing the ridge, the trail crosses Chimney Top Road. Pick up the trail on the other side of the gravel road, across the parking lot, and behind the kiosk.

From here, the trail descends for about 0.5 miles, before crossing Chimney Top Creek. Note that Koomer Ridge Trail #220 comes in on your left, but stay right on #221. Cross the creek once again and this time bear left to stay on #221 (again, see Map 2). The Sheltowee Trace #100 will join #221 from the north, so for the next several miles you will see both a white diamond and a turtle blazing the trail. Sheltowee, meaning "Big Turtle," was

Bridge over Parched Corn Creek. the name given to Daniel Boone by

Map 2: Swift Camp Creek to Chimney Top Creek

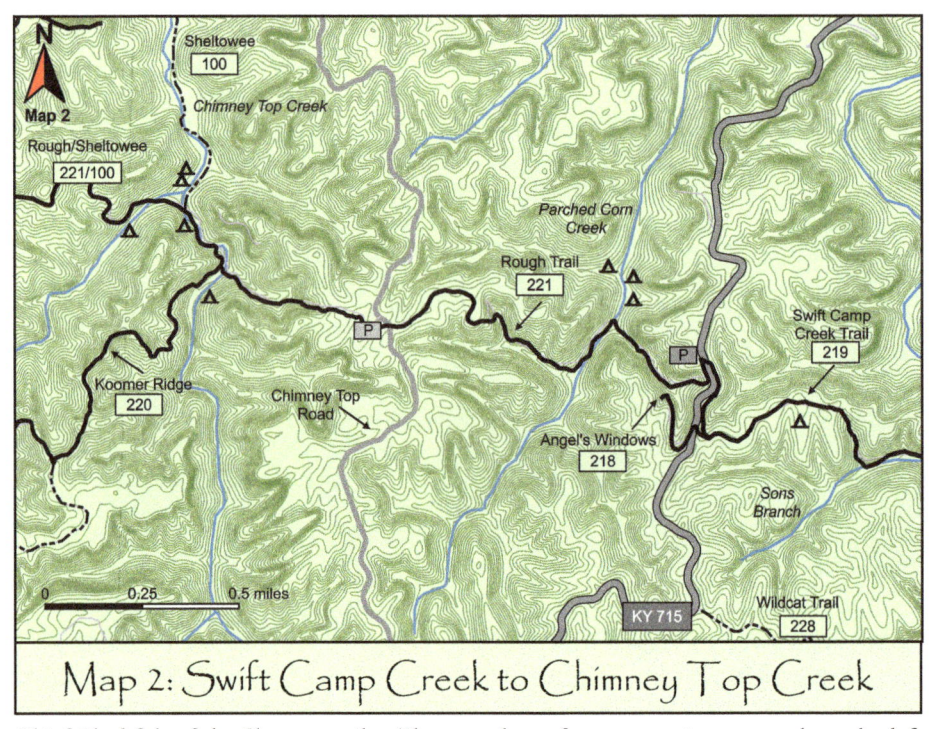

Chief Blackfish of the Shawnee tribe. There are lots of great camping spots where the left and right forks of Chimney Top Creek join.

Continuing hiking west on trails #221/100, cross the creek again, and then crossover the Left Fork of Chimney Top Creek. Over the next 1.25 miles, the trail climbs atop a nice ridge with commanding views, before crossing Signature Rock with more views to the east. In just a bit, both Sheltowee Trace #100 and Pinch 'Em Tight Trail #223 take off to the left (west). But stay right (north) on Rough Trail #221. (See Map 3)

At this point, you must decide if you want to take the 2.4-mile out-and-back spur to Hanson's Point. This is not a marked trail and requires working your way along a narrow path through 12 to 15-foot pine trees. But the reward at the end is spectacular views of both Chimney Top Rock and Half Moon Rock.

View from Hanson's Point.

… Red River Gorge

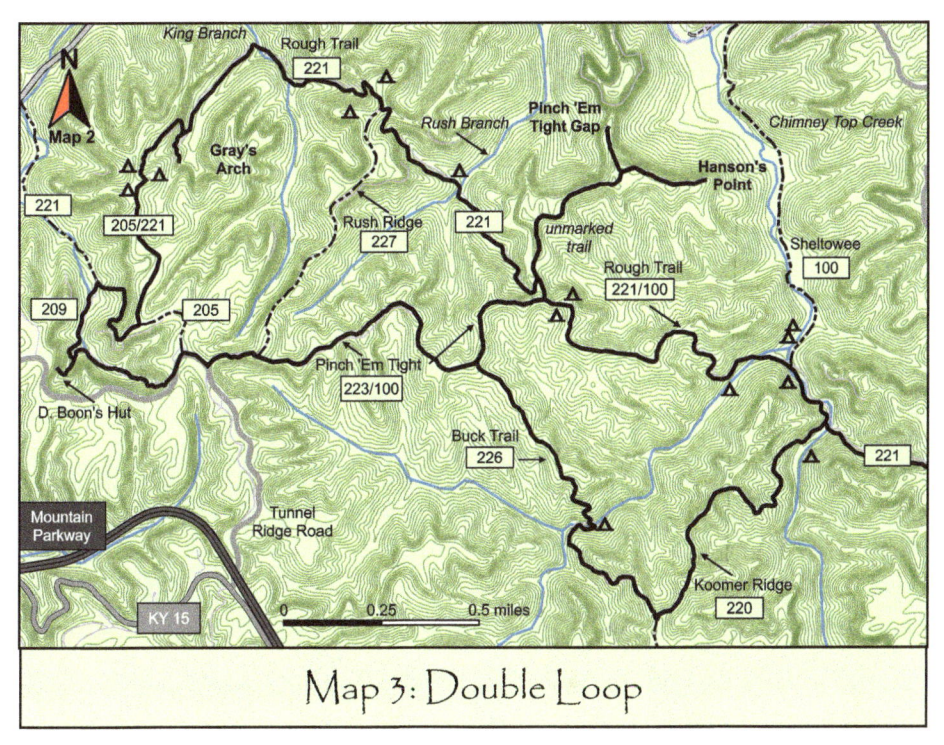

Map 3: Double Loop

To find the path, continue right on Rough Trail #221 for several yards. On your right you will see a narrow, but defined trail heading north atop a pine-covered ridge. There are several large campsites on these ridges, with spectacular views and night-time skies, but no water is available.

It is slightly less than 1.0 mile to the far eastern tip of Hanson's Point. Surprisingly, you can hear both the gurgle of Chimney Top Creek and the whoosh of the Red River 300-vertical feet below where you stand. The fall colors here can be brilliant. Another short spur takes you north over to Pinch 'Em Tight Gap, but the backcountry campers have not always practiced the best housekeeping skills.

Returning to Rough Trail #221, bear right to immediately descend past a pair of small rockshelters with an interesting bench rock formation seen off-trail on your left. Just a wee bit further down the trail is a nice plunging waterfall, also on your left, with some equally beautiful rock formations. Both of these sights are well worth the time checking out.

The best camping spot to be had is at the next creek crossing at Rush Branch. Just downstream is a really sweet campsite that is great if you can snag it. Otherwise you'll have to continue along #221 and climb ridgetop to find flat spots off the trail. But let's assume this is your lucky day and you get to camp along Rush Creek.

Day 3: Rush Branch to Chimney Top Creek—8.0 miles
Rough Trail #221/Gray's Arch Trail #205 – 3.2 miles
D. Boon Hut Trail #209 – 0.8 miles
Pinch 'Em Tight Trail #223 – 1.2 miles
Buck Trail #226 – 1.5 miles
Koomer Ridge Trail #220 – 1.25 miles

After packing up your gear and topping off your water bottles, continue heading northwest on Rough Trail #221, past Corrosion Cave (on your right) and Second Story (on your left). As noted previously, there are several camping places just beyond here, all ridgetop and none with water. Rush Ridge Trail #227 will come in on your left, but bear right to stay on Rough Trail.

In a little over a mile you'll reach the short spur on your left to Gray's Arch. This is a totally cool place to explore, despite the relatively large number of people who day hike here. Take lots of time–arches like this are what the Gorge is known for. Besides, you'll need to rest up to climb all the stairs getting out of here.

Gray's Arch

At Gray's Arch the trail changes name to (drum roll, please) Gray's Arch Trail (#205). Once you climb out of the drainage, it's an easy mile to the junction of Gray's Arch Trail (#205) and Rough Trail (#221). Turn right (southwest) on Rough Trail, hike 0.5 miles, and then turn left (south) on D. Boon Hut Trail (#209). In about 0.4 miles, you will see a small spur on your right (south side of the trail) leading to a large rockshelter with remnants of what *some* believe to be Daniel's winter get-away. With ten kids at home, he probably enjoyed the peace and quiet found here. This is also the site of an old mine where potassium nitrate was leached from the sandstone for use in making gunpowder during the War of 1812.

Continuing on the D. Boon Hut Trail, you'll have another 0.4 miles and two flights of stairs to climb up to Tunnel Ridge Road. Hang a left on the gravel road and walk for about ten minutes until you see the sign on your left for the Sheltowee Trace and Pinch 'Em Tight Trail (#100 and 223, respectively). Duck back into the woods and head east.

Follow #223/100 past the junction with trail #227, for about 1.25 miles. Then bear right (south) on Buck Trail #226 for 1.5 miles. A left (north) turn on Koomer Ridge Trail #220 will take you back to Rough Trail #221. This sounds totally confusing. But with a good map and sense of direction you'll find your way.

Red River Gorge

You should now be back in the upper reaches of Chimney Top Creek, looking for a nice campsite with water availability. There is a really sweet spot just downstream (north) of the intersection of #220 and 221, on the other side of the creek.

Day 4: Chimney Top Creek to Rock Bridge Picnic Area—9.6 miles
Rough Trail #221 – 2.25 miles
Swift Camp Creek Trail #219 – 6.8 miles
Rock Bridge Trail #207 – 0.5 miles

From here it should all be familiar territory. Head east on Rough Trail #221, cross over KY 715, and then pick up Swift Camp Creek Trail #219. A 0.5-mile hike up the Rock Bridge Loop Trail #207 should bring you back to your vehicle.

Pink Lady Slippers are prolific in the Gorge.

Side Trips: Several of the Gorge's more popular sights are within easy driving distance and require only short walks, including Chimney Top, Sky Bridge, and Nada Tunnel. The Gladie Visitor Center, a combination of living history, folklore, and mother nature, is also worth a stop.

Remember passing Sky Bridge Station? In addition to gourmet dogs, they also serve ice cream and cold beer. And just on the other side of the Mountain Parkway, only a few miles from Red River Gorge, is Natural Bridge State Resort Park. In addition to hiking opportunities, they have soft beds, hot showers, and southern fare. Might be worth considering. parks.ky.gov/parks/resortparks/natural-bridge/

Other good-eatin' choices include the popular Red River Rockhouse and Miguel's. Read the Auxier Ridge hike for more information on both of these fine eateries. Yum.

Rockcastle River

The 55-mile Rockcastle River, named for its castle-like rock formations, is a tributary of the Cumberland River in southern Kentucky. In most places, the river is only 60- to 80-feet wide and ranges from crystal blue between mid-summer and late winter, before becoming lightly muddied with spring rains. Whitewater paddlers know the 5-mile class III-IV, section of the Rockcastle River just above Bee Rock Campground as the "Narrows." The Daniel Boone National Forest encompasses the river and the surrounding area.

Two backpacking loop options are offered up—one on the east (Vanhook Falls) and the other on the west (Bee Rock) side of the river. These two loops can be combined, as described below. The eastern loop also lies within the Cane Creek Wilderness Area. In addition, The Nature Conservancy owns about 1,900 acres within the Rockcastle River watershed, to further protect the pristine waters and endangered species living in the region.

Rock wall near Van Hook Falls.

Regulations: Dispersed (backcountry) camping is permitted in the Daniel Boone National Forest (DBNF). No permit is required. Proper food and trash storage should be practiced, using bear canisters (vaults) or proper hanging techniques. In this part of the DBNF, all camping must be 100 feet away from the base of any cliff or rockshelter. Be sure to practice "Leave No Trace" principles. Pets are permitted, but if requested by a Forest Service Officer, should be restrained. For more information, see tinyurl.com/CampingDBNF.

Rockcastle River:
20. Rockcastle Narrows West—Bee Rock to Beech Creek

An easy overnighter with the opportunity to join the Vanhook Falls side of the Rockcastle River.

Trail Length: 7 miles; 15.7 miles if combined with the Rockcastle Narrows East Trails
Suggested Time: 2 days / 1 night
Map: US Forest Service: tinyurl.com/RockcastleNarrows

Overview: The trail climbs to Bee Rock, a bluff overlooking the Rockcastle River, before descending back to the river and a quiet campsite along Beech Creek. This overnighter loop can be combined with trails on the other side of the Rockcastle River to make a 15.7-mile double loop.

Directions: From I-75, take exit #38 for London. Turn right (west) on KY 192. Travel 18 miles. Just before crossing the Rockcastle River, turn right into the Bee Rock Picnic Area and Campground (Forest Service Road 624). Park near Sublimity Bridge, on the south (Laurel County) side of the river.

Staging: Bee Rock Campground is located at the trailhead. The Pulaski County (north) side of the campground has 19 sites and is open mid-April through mid-October. The Laurel County (south) side of the campground has 9 sites and is open year-round. Both sides have potable water, except during the winter season, and vault toilets. Fees are $8 single campsite; $12 for a double. No reservations.

Route Description: This hike combines the Bee Rock Loop Trail #529, the Rockcastle Narrows Trail #503, and the Beach Narrows Trail to form a 7-mile loop, including the spur to Beech Creek. Many hikers do this as a day-hike, but the beauty of the river and the solitude found at Beech Creek make this a good overnighter.

To begin the hike, walk over Sublimity Bridge (closed to vehicular traffic) until you're on the north side of the river. Built by the Civilian Conservation Corp in the 1930s, the rock foundation of Sublimity Bridge is a beautiful piece of work. Once across the bridge, turn left (west) and walk the paved road for about 0.25 miles, until you see the trailhead on your right.

Wait a minute. Did you say Sublimity Bridge? Maybe before we start hiking we should start with a short story. And the area around the Rockcastle River is full of interesting tidbits of trivia that has the inherent danger of both astounding your friends and boring your enemies.

In the mid-1800s, the Rockcastle River was the site of several resort hotels that attracted visitors from hundreds of miles around with claims of medicinal springs, fine dining, comfortable lodging, and enticing entertainment. The largest and best known of these was the Rockcastle Springs Resort Hotel, located about seven miles downstream at the confluence of the Rockcastle and Cumberland rivers.

Rockcastle Narrows West

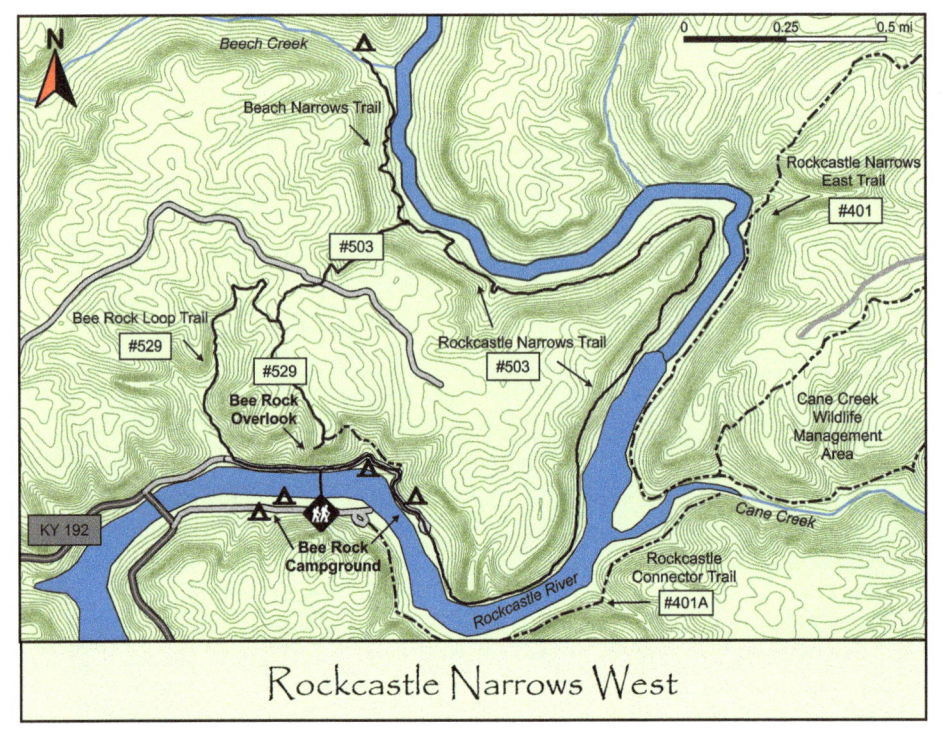

Another resort was built around 1850 by Dr. Christopher Columbus "C.C." Graham on the Pulaski County side of what is now Bee Rock Campground and was known as the Sublimity Springs Resort Hotel. In addition to the hotel, Dr. Graham built slave quarters, horse stables, a gristmill, and a sawmill along the river. (Dr. Graham has mistakenly been credited with creating graham flour, but we truly digress.) The resort, which operated for about 30 years, charged a daily rate of 75 cents or $5 per week.

About a mile upriver from the Sublimity Bridge, the Warner Hotel stood at the confluence of the Rockcastle River and Cane Creek. A two-story structure, built entirely of chestnut wood, the resort operated until the early 1900s. Scant evidence of the hotel's remains can be seen along the Rockcastle Narrows East Trail (#401) on the Laurel County side of the river.

Now let's get hiking. After crossing Sublimity Bridge and turning left, walk about five minutes on the road until you see the trailhead on your right for the Bee Rock Loop Trail #529, marked with white diamonds. The trail begins with a steady climb for about 0.5-miles, along a small creek graced with several seasonal waterfalls and interesting rock formations. From here, the trail then crosses a small wooden bridge and continues to bear east for a short distance, before meeting the Rockcastle Narrows Trail #503.

Turn right (south) and stay on the ridgetop Bee Rock Loop Trail. In about 0.4-miles, you will pass through a thicket of mountain laurel (beautiful in early summer) and an unmarked trail will appear on your left. This is the continuation of the Bee Rock Loop Trail, but continue walking straight (yes, still south) for another five minutes to take the short spur to the Bee Rock Overlook, which commands a splendid view of the Rockcastle River. More evidence of the Civilian Conservation Corp can be seen here with the old stone walls and pillars.

Rockcastle River

Hmmm. Bee Rock? There must be another story here… and there is one. Legend has it that huge colonies of wild bees were living in the eroded sandstone that forms the bluffs overlooking the Rockcastle River. Well, these feral bees were messing with the local farmer's hives, introducing disease to the European strains, and adversely impacting pollination efforts and honey yields. Around the turn of the last century, a couple of young fellows threw a few sticks of dynamite into the crevices atop the bluff and folklore has it that honey came aburstin' outta' that rock and flowed all the way to the river. You can't make this stuff up. And yes, sometimes truth is stranger than fiction.

From the Bee Rock Overlook, retrace your steps north about 0.5 miles, back to where the Rockcastle Narrows Trail #503 joined the #529 trail, taking care NOT to turn right onto the Bee Rock Loop Trail. After backtracking your steps, continue straight on #503. Look for a small downed tree with a red paint patch, partially blocking the trail. (This tree has been here for years and let's hope it's still there when you try to navigate with these directions.) The Rockcastle Narrows Trail is not well-marked at this point, but take a close look at the map and you should be alright. Trail #529 is blazed with red diamonds that after so much UV light exposure, the blazes look more dark orange in color.

After a few minutes of hiking you will come to a paved road that leads to a private farm. Cross the road to stay on the Rockcastle Narrows Trail. The path soon descends along a natural rock wall, with a nice rock house and an intermittent wet-weather waterfall. After briefly traversing a wooded area, the trail takes a long, but gentle, descent down to the Rockcastle River.

Continue along the Rockcastle Narrows Trail until you near the river. Turn left (north) on the Beach Narrows Trail to Beech Creek (yes, the spelling is accurate!) This section of the Rockcastle River is known as "The Narrows" due to a narrowing of the riverbed and the large rocks that form a small, but significant, series of rapids. "The Narrows" has flipped many a flat-water canoeist and provided lots of excitement for whitewater boaters. There are a few great lunch spots found here on the huge boulders overlooking the river.

Rockcastle River, just downstream of the whitewater section known as "The Narrows".

Backpacking Kentucky

The US Forest Service has not maintained the Beach Narrows Trail in recent years, but it is fairly easy to follow. In about 0.8 miles you will reach Beech Creek and a nice campsite on the opposite side of the stream. Few people camp here any more, but there is plenty of flat space and an old fire pit. The stream itself is beautiful to explore and provides lots of fresh water year round.

The return hike along the Beach Narrows Trail will take you back to the Rockcastle Narrows Trail, which then follows the river downstream for about 2.5 more miles. Along the way, be sure to notice the towering sandstone bluffs on your right. Once back to the campground, continue walking along the paved road until you reach the Sublimity Bridge.

Sublimity Bridge with Bee Rock in the background.

Side Trip: If you want to make a longer trip out of this trail, see the next section on Vanhook Falls and the Rockcastle Narrows East Loop. After hiking the Bee Rock portion and crossing Sublimity Bridge back to the south side of the campground, turn left on the road to find the Rockcastle Connector trailhead. From here it is about 1.25 miles to Cane Creek. There is not a bridge at Cane Creek and at high water difficult to cross. But once spring rains subside, hikers can usually safely wade the stream.

Once on the Rockcastle Narrows East Trail, follow the Vanhook Falls description to make a 6.2-mile loop by utilizing a short section of the Sheltowee Trace. The Vanhook loop will add a total of 8.7 miles to your backpacking adventure (the 6.2-mile loop, plus out-and-back on the Connector Trail, which is 1.25 miles each way.) Backcountry campsites are marked on the Vanhook map.

Rockcastle River:
21. Rockcastle Narrows East—Vanhook Falls

An easy hike to Vanhook Falls, followed by a more rigorous loop hike to the top of a ridge and then down to the Rockcastle River and Cane Creek.

Trail Length: 11.6 miles
Suggested Time: 2 days / 1 night
Maps: US Forest Service: tinyurl.com/VanHook
US Forest Service: tinyurl.com/RockNarrowEast

Overview: The easy out-and-back hike to Vanhook Falls is a popular day trip, particularly after spring rains. The loop portion of this overnighter takes you ridgetop, before dropping back down to follow the Rockcastle River. Backcountry camping is available right on the river. The trail then follows Cane Creek, returning you back to the falls area.

Directions: From I-75 south, take exit #38 for London. Turn right (west) onto KY 192. Drive 14.0 miles to the intersection of KY 192 W and KY 1193 S. A large gravel parking lot will be on your left. To reach the trailhead, carefully cross back over KY 192 to the north side of the road. The trail begins on the Sheltowee Trace Trail #100.

Staging: There is a backcountry campsite a little more than 1.0 mile from the trailhead, just off the Sheltowee Trace. Camping is also available farther down KY 192 (west of the TH) at Bee Rock Campground. Holly Bay Campground, situated on Laurel River Lake, is less than 10 minutes south of the trailhead. Holly Bay is a full-service facility and fills quickly in the summer and on weekends.

Route Description:
Sheltowee Trace #100—3.9 miles
Rockcastle Narrows East Trail #401—5 miles
Sheltowee Trace #100—2.7 miles

Vanhook Falls lies in the heart of the nearly 6,700-acre Cane Creek Wilderness Management Area in the Daniel Boone National Forest. Several smaller tributaries, including Rooks, Laurel, Upper and Lower Pounder, Vanhook, and Grassy Branch, all converge in the Cane Creek drainage before flowing into the Rockcastle River.

This balloon-loop overnighter begins on the other side of KY 192 from the parking lot. You'll follow the Sheltowee Trace #100 north, as the trail passes under towering hemlocks, making its way along scenic Pounder Branch. With the exception of the last 100 yards, the trail is wide and flat to rolling. There are multiple smaller waterfalls along the way, with at least two creek crossings and some rock hopping required. Despite these alluring attributes, the trail to Vanhook Falls is typically quiet and peaceful most of the time.

Approximately 2 miles from the trailhead, you'll see a small rogue trail off to your left that leads up to a small campsite, and just past that a small sandstone outcropping.

Backpacking Kentucky

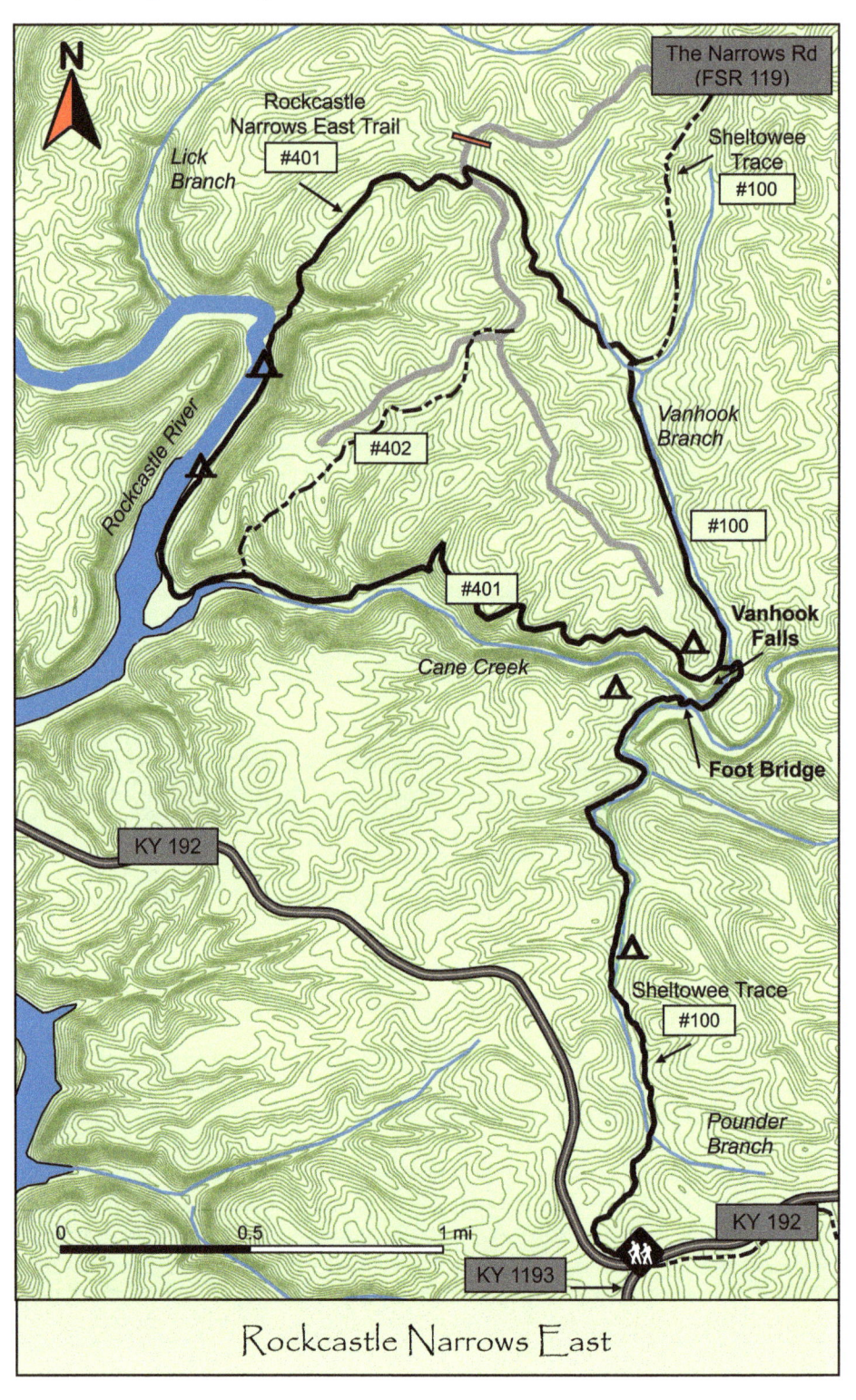

Rockcastle Narrows East

Rockcastle River

Footbridge over Cane Creek.

Here the trail takes a brief, but steep descent into the confluence of Pounder Branch and Cane Creek, with two wooden footbridges crossing each waterway in succession. The large flat rocks along Cane Creek make a beautiful lunch spot overlooking the lively rapid where the footbridge crosses over. From this vantage point, the placid Cane Creek begins pouring through a series of large boulder gardens as the creek tumbles into the Rockcastle River about two miles downstream.

Cross over Cane Creek and walk another 0.1 mile along the Sheltowee Trace, beginning a slow ascent up the Vanhook Branch drainage. The trail follows under a nice rock overhang before climbing swiftly to a good view of the 40-foot Vanhook Falls. A spur trail on your left drops down to the backside of the falls, allowing hikers lots of beautiful photo ops. In August of 2016, a sturdy group of volunteers built a wooden staircase that leads to the falls, reducing the environmental impact of all who hike here.

After experiencing the joy of falling water, return to the main trail and bear left to hike above the falls. The creek upstream of the falls also provides some pretty views of the drainage. Just on the other (west) side of Vanhook Branch,

Vanhook Falls after a summer rain.

the loop portion of this hike begins. Stay right, heading north on the Sheltowee Trace #100 for another 1.25 miles. Right where Yuel and Vanhook Branch meet, the Sheltowee continues northeast (to the right), but you will want to take the left trail (heading northwest) to pick up the Rockcastle Narrows East Trail #401.

From the trail split, #401 climbs ridgetop until you reach gravel road FSR 119. Bear left (south) on this road for just a few minutes until you see the trail again on your right (west of the road). The trail follows an old roadbed for about 0.25 miles—in late spring, this is your best opportunity for finding pink lady slippers. The trail then bears left and it's mostly downhill to the Rockcastle River. Be sure to check out the tall, narrow waterfall on trail-left, about halfway down the hill. You'll have to set your camera/phone on vertical panoramic to fit it all in.

Once you reach the Rockcastle, you can begin looking for a campsite on the right side of the trail, between you and the river. There are several sandy places, with lots of driftwood for an evening fire. If the weather and your skills permit, a swim might be a great way to wash the day's grime off your skin. However, in spring after heavy rains the Rockcastle becomes quite swollen and these campsites wash out. If so, your next best place to camp is further downstream, also on the right side of the trail. A small spur leads under a nice group of pines to a large flat area, complete with fire pit. You will be situated just above the last rapid of what constitutes "The Narrows" of the Rockcastle River, a nice but relatively short whitewater run.

The next morning, continue hiking south along the Rockcastle Narrows East Trail #401, until you reach Cane Creek. In the late 1800s, the Warner Hotel stood at the confluence of the Rockcastle River and Cane Creek. A two-story structure built entirely of chestnut wood, the resort operated until the early 1900s. If you explore around a little bit, you'll find evidence of where the hotel was located.

From here the trail turns sharply east. After passing Winding Stair Gap Trail #402 (unmarked as of this writing), you'll have a few short climbs ahead of you. In about 2 miles, you'll see several spur trails leading to a small campsite on your left. This spot is also a decent location for a base camp, if you want to set up camp here and day hike the area. Just past this last campsite, you will reach Vanhook Branch again, just above the falls. Bear right (south) on the Sheltowee and trace your steps back to the parking lot.

Side Trip: If you're up for a little fishing, Cane Creek is stocked annually with 3,750 rainbow trout, equally distributed across the months of 3, 4, 5, 6 and 10. A catch and release (no harvest) season applies October 1 – March 31. All other fishing regulations and permit requirements apply. Smallmouth fishing is also excellent at the confluence of Cane Creek and the Rockcastle River.

Vireo nest found near Vanhook Falls.

Sheltowee Trace National Recreation Trail

The Sheltowee Trace was established within the Daniel Boone National Forest (DBNF) in 1979. Inspired by the Appalachian Trail, the trail was originally designed by Verne Orndorff, a landscape architect with the USDA Forest Service. Verne passed away in June 2016 at 100 years of age. What an amazing legacy he left for all of us to enjoy!

Currently, the Sheltowee is 323 miles long, end to end. Even better, the Sheltowee keeps growing. The Trace now runs the entire length of the DBNF and extends into the Big South Fork National Recreation Area, which straddles the Kentucky/Tennessee border. The northern terminus of the trail begins just north of Morehead, KY and the southern terminus lies north of Robbins, TN.

The Sheltowee is a linear trail, with multiple access points. Although other trails within the DBNF can be utilized to create some loop options, these are few and far between. Further, the Sheltowee relies on many local roads, both paved and graveled, to join various sections together. And some sections are multi-use, allowing horses, ATVs, and mountain bikers to share the trail with hikers. Yes, there are some drawbacks to this trail. But the Sheltowee also weaves together some of the most spectacular scenery in the DBNF, including many of the natural arches, waterfalls, overlooks, and sparkling streams found in the region.

It's important to realize that the Sheltowee Trace is not always its own unique trail. Huh? Frequently, the Sheltowee is actually an overlay on other trails in the DBNF, Red River Gorge or the Big South Fork. For example, the Moonbow Trail running from Cumberland Falls to Bark Camp Creek Cascades is also a part of the Sheltowee Trace.

It was a bit tough to decide on the organization of the trails highlighted in this book. Both the Red River Gorge Geological Area and the Big South Fork Recreation Area lie in the DBNF. And the Sheltowee Trace runs through all of them. Consequently, some "Sheltowee Trace" trails are listed as Big South Fork or Red River Gorge hikes if they fall within those parks. Otherwise, Sheltowee trails are listed below as "Sheltowee Trace National Recreation Trails" if they are simply in the DBNF. Confusing, yes. But don't worry too much about it.

Regulations: No permits or fees are required to hike the Sheltowee Trace through the DBNF. Dispersed (aka backcountry) camping is permitted in the Daniel Boone National Forest (DBNF). Proper food and trash storage should be practiced, using bear canisters (vaults) or proper hanging techniques. In this part of the DBNF, all camping must be 100 feet away from the base of any cliff or rockshelter. Be sure to practice "Leave No Trace" principles. Pets are permitted on the Sheltowee, but should be restrained if requested by a Forest Service Officer.

As noted above, the Sheltowee Trace also traverses land within the Red River Gorge and the Big South Fork. Please see regulations elsewhere in this book pertaining to those areas. More information can be found at tinyurl.com/DBNFrules or tinyurl.com/CampingDBNF.

Sheltowee Trace National Recreation Trail:
22. Bark Camp Creek to Dog Slaughter Falls

The canine lover's choice, as long as Rover can't read the signs.

Trail Length: 10.9 miles one-way; 21.8 miles round-trip (out-and-back)
Suggested Time: 2 days / 1 night; 3 days / 2 nights
Maps: US Forest Service: tinyurl.com/BarkCampTrail
US Forest Service: tinyurl.com/DogSlaughterTrail
Sheltowee Trace National Recreation Trail (maps 7 and 8): goo.gl/BoRiJh
OutrageGIS.com: Sheltowee Trace Map—South

Overview: Two beautiful creek hikes are linked together by a portion of the Sheltowee Trace, also known as the Moonbow Trail. This backpack can be done as an out-and-back. Alternately, shuttle can be run for a great overnighter. Either way, highlights include Bark Camp Creek Cascades, Star Creek Falls, Dog Slaughter Falls, multiple rockhouses, and views of the Cumberland River.

Directions:
To Bark Camp Creek trailhead: From I-75 exit #25 at Corbin, follow US 25 W for 4.7 miles. Turn right on KY 1193. Drive another 4.6 miles. Stay straight on KY 1277 where KY 1193 bears to the right. (KY 1277 is known as Bee Creek Road on some maps, but is not physically marked as such.) Drive 1.2 miles. You will see a slightly misleading, brown Forest Service sign for FS 88 and State Hwy 90 on your right. Immediately past the sign, turn left on graveled Forest Service Road 193. In 1.7 miles the road will cross Bark Camp Creek. This is your TH. Shoulder parking is available for 4-5 cars.

To Dog Slaughter trailhead: From I-75 exit #25 at Corbin, follow US 25 W for 7.5 miles. Bear right on KY 90 W. Drive an additional 2.3 miles. Turn right on Forest Service Road 195. The trailhead will be 0.8 miles down this gravel road.

Staging: You can camp anywhere in the Daniel Boone National Forest, per the regulations outlined previously. Just a few miles away from Dog Slaughter Creek, a full-service campground is available at Cumberland Falls State Resort Park.

Route Description: (all distances are one-way)
Bark Camp Trail—2.6 miles
Sheltowee Trace (Moonbow Trail)—4.3 miles
Dog Slaughter Trail—4 miles

Canine lovers unite! Make no bones about it—despite their names, the water in both creeks runs clear and gorgeous. This is a beautiful little gem of a hike, popular with locals and non-natives alike. Admittedly, the reported mileage estimates of all three trails vary somewhat.

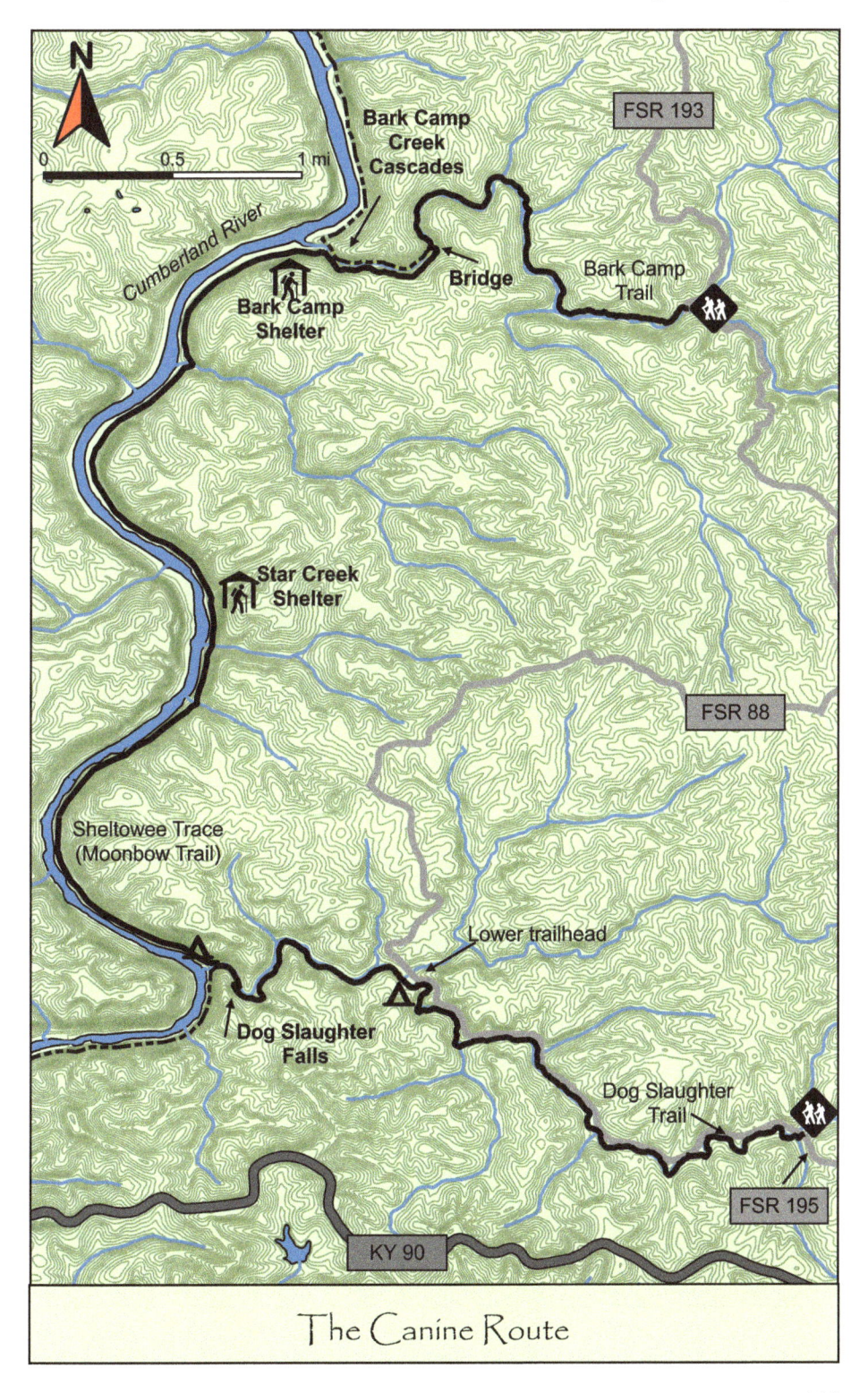

Sheltowee Trace

The Canine Route

Backpacking Kentucky

Even the Forest Service signs vary from their maps. But no worries. You'll soon lose track of time walking along these trails.

Your backcountry adventure can start from either trailhead, but the route described below assumes you begin at Bark Camp Creek. If you run shuttle, Google has a decent map of the gravel-road maze that links the two trailheads. (All gravel roads are not shown on the accompanying map.)

FS 193 crosses Bark Camp Creek where the stocking truck releases rainbows and browns each year in months 3, 4, 5, 6 and 10. As you might suspect, this is a great place for locals to go for carryout fish. So sometimes the trailhead gets a little messy. But in no time the hike quickly turns almost pristine, and what makes this creek great for trout, makes it great for hiking. The spring-fed waters stay cool and clear year-round, with towering hemlocks providing lots of soothing shade.

Bark Camp Trail #413 follows the creek as it flows west for 2.6 miles, passing several nice camp spots and rockhouses, while traversing lush rhododendron thickets. About 2 miles from the trailhead, a new bridge reroutes the trail to the left side of the creek. The old bridge, located further downstream, had washed out one time too many. You can either cross the new bridge to stay on trail #413, or you can continue straight on creek-right, only to later boulder-hop back across the creek just below Bark Camp Creek Cascades.

The trail joins the Sheltowee Trace trail at the Cumberland River, just below the cascades. Following the Sheltowee a short distance further west will lead you to the Bark Camp Creek Shelter, available for an overnighter or a hot fire on a cold day. Follow the spur trail to your left, away from the river, to find the three-sided shelter. If you want, you can pitch a tent or hang a hammock here if sleeping inside the shelter is not your thing.

From there, the trail follows the Cumberland River upstream. This section of the Sheltowee Trace #100 is known as the Moonbow Trail and runs all the way to Cumberland Falls. Unfortunately, a considerable amount of trash floats down the river and accumulates on the banks below. Despite the Park Service's gallant efforts to carry tremendous

Bark Camp Creek Cascades. (K. Rose)

tonnage to the landfill, an inordinate number of plastic bottles and other rubbish get washed up after every good rain.

In another 2 miles, the Sheltowee Trace passes the Star Creek Shelter, also a decent place to spend the night. The shelter is not easily seen from the trail, so be on the lookout for a small path leading to the shelter, fire pit, and outhouse. On the opposite side of the trail, a small sandy beach is located on the riverbank. Also be sure to check out the small tributary just north of the shelter and the small footpath that leads to Star Creek Falls. Here the water pours over a sandstone ledge to form a thin 60-foot plunge-style waterfall.

About 200 yards past Star Creek Shelter, continuing upstream along the Sheltowee, the trail passes under Rock Fall Arch. Here you'll find two boulders of Herculean strength on either side of the trail supporting a third rock that traverses overhead. In a little over 2 miles, the trail crosses over a very scenic wooden bridge that traverses Dog Slaughter Creek. The view here is quite nice. Just downstream of where the creek flows into the Cumberland River, there is a sandy beach area that many campers use for overnighters.

Staying on the main trail, cross the bridge and bear sharp right as you climb up a short ascent. Here the Sheltowee continues upstream and Dog Slaughter Trail bears left (east). Scramble over a few rock ledges, follow the trail back down the other side, cross under a rockhouse, and in a few minutes you'll hear the sound of Dog Slaughter Falls. Most of the creek is spring-fed, guaranteeing you a waterfall show year-round. Some argue that springtime after a heavy rain is the best time to see the 15- to 20-foot falls, but the colors of autumn reflecting in the still pool below the falls is unbeatable.

Bridge over Dog Slaughter Creek.

There are several stories circulating as to how the creek and falls got its name, none of them very pleasant and most highly imaginative. And rarely do you ever see any of the explanations printed in tourism brochures. You can use the margins of this page to add your own lore.

After enjoying the falls, continue along the creek-side trail for another mile until you see another wooden bridge crossing Dog Slaughter Creek on your left. The bridge takes you to a lower trailhead that some people use to minimize the distance, thus the joy, of hiking to the falls. While there is a campsite between this bridge and the gravel road FSR 195, the better campsite is just ahead on the right side of the trail. Walking east along Dog Slaughter Trail for another 3 miles or less, and you'll arrive at the upper trailhead, also on FSR 195.

The upper section of the trail is really pretty, as it follows the narrow creek through clouds of rhododendron and stately hemlock, occasionally giving way to beech, magnolia, paw paw, and spice bush. Here the creek murmurs quietly, like an intimate couple at a French café. However, the gravel road parallels the trail on the other side of the creek and every time a car passes you do hear some crunching noises of rubber hitting rock, like an elderly man clearing his throat. But, in mid-summer the filtered light is stunning and you won't run into many people on the trail between the upper and lower trailheads.

If you've run shuttle, you should find your vehicle here. If not, sit down and enjoy the scenery. Grab your water bottle and a snack. And contemplate how different the trail always looks when you head back the other way.

Side Trip: From the upper Dog Slaughter Creek trailhead you are about 15 to 20 minutes from Cumberland Falls. The stone and beam construction of DuPont Lodge is pretty cool and the food decent. Grab a window seat with views of the river and order that Kentucky Hot Brown. And the nearby trail to Eagle Falls, at around 2.5 miles round-trip, is also worth the hike.

Bear, tentatively hiking at Dog Slaughter Creek.

Sheltowee Trace National Recreation Trail: 23. Barren Fork

Rodney, you were right. This section of the Sheltowee Trace has "unexpected beauty."

Trail Length: 9 miles one-way; 18 miles round-trip
Suggested Time: 2 days / 1 night; 3 days / 2 nights
Maps: US Forest Service: tinyurl.com/Barren-Fork
US Forest Service: tinyurl.com/STT-30
OutrageGIS: tinyurl.com/STT-South

Overview: An easy overnighter, the Barren Fork section of the Sheltowee Trace runs between US 27 and KY 700, just north of Whitley City. You can set-up shuttle and hike it one-way, or do it as an out-and-back. Better yet, try and sweet-talk someone into dropping you off at one end, and picking you up on the other side.

This pocket of magic holds rock houses, rock shelters, rock walls, and rock overhangs, all tied together with gentle trails lined with ferns, moss and spring wildflowers. There are two forks in the trail, but the choice is easy. The trail descends along Railroad Fork, before joining Barren Fork, and finally Indian Creek. The shade is deep and there's water almost every step of the way. Breathe in the good, clean smell of the organic matter created, in part, by the hemlocks, rhododendron, and umbrella magnolias that dominate this beautifully-serene area.

Directions:
To the US 27 trailhead: Find Whitley City on your Kentucky map, located about 30 miles south of Somerset, KY. Just north of town is the Stearns Ranger Station for the Daniel Boone National Forest. About 1.1 miles north of the ranger station is the trailhead. Park in the gravel lot on the eastern side of the highway.

To the KY 700 trailhead: From north of Whitley City, take KY 700 east for 6.8 miles. You'll see a gravel road on your left, county road 1050, but it's also marked as Catron Road or Needle Road on some maps. The Sheltowee Trace crosses KY 700 here. There is no parking lot of any kind, but you can park on the shoulder just south of the trailhead. However, this is not the best place to leave a vehicle overnight.

Staging: Barren Fork Horse Camp is located just east of the Ranger Station, off Barren Fork Road. Neigh, you don't need to bring a horse. Rates are $8 per night; $12 for two nights. Potable water, vault toilets, picnic tables, and large grassy areas for pitching a tent are available. Both hoot and screech owls are willing and able to serenade you at night.

Route Description: The hike follows the Sheltowee Trace the entire time, although multiple other trails intersect from both north and south. Although horses are permitted on most of the trails, damage from these impressive beasts is minimal and the trails are a

Backpacking Kentucky

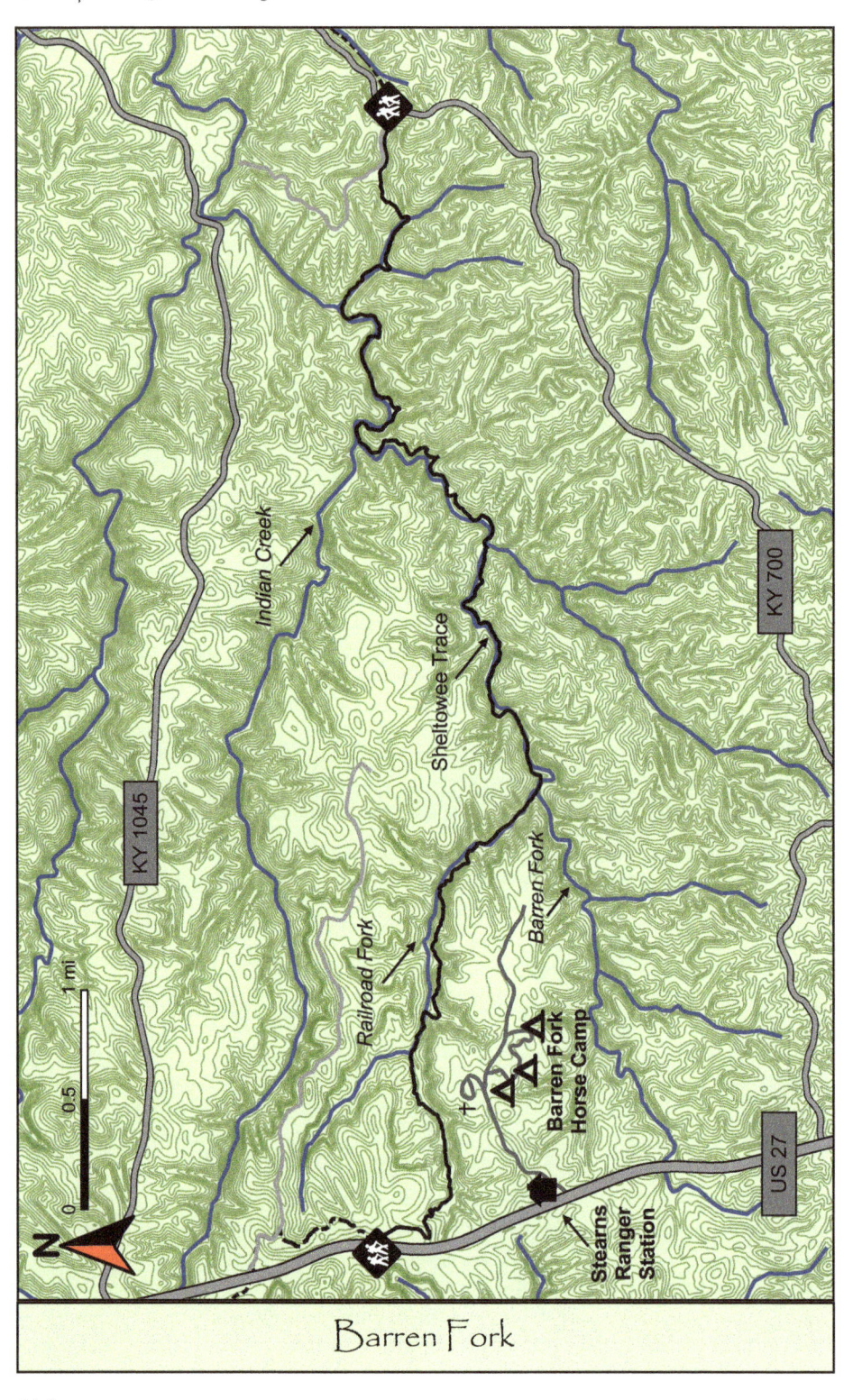

Barren Fork

delight to hike. In most places the trail is wide, allowing side-by-side hiking, and good camping spots are scattered throughout the hike. The canopy is high overhead, with little understory to harbor ticks and mosquitoes. You are rarely away from one creek or another, so water is always close at hand.

As noted above, you can easily hike this as an out-and-back. But there are also some opportunities to make a balloon configuration using either the Belgian Loop and North Flat Rock Trails, or some of the trails that lead from Barren Fork Horse Camp. Use the map links noted above if you are interested in other options.

But let's assume you start at the western trailhead, located off US 27, for an out-and-back overnighter. After leaving the trailhead parking lot, turn right (south) on the Sheltowee Trace. In about 0.3 miles, the trail ducks under some power lines. Bear east here and head towards the small rock ledges on your left. (Don't follow the Draft Trail.)

In another mile, the Flat Rock Ridge Trail (#616) comes in on your left. Stay straight on the Sheltowee. The next 0.5 miles of hiking follows Railroad Fork down to where the trail crosses a small tributary. Just past the other side of the wood footbridge, on your left, is an old stone foundation leftover from the remains of a small trestle, remnants of the coal industry that thrived in this area many years ago. Not far from here you'll pass the first of two mine shafts found along the trail. Both shafts are mere horizontal slits in the base of rock overhangs, each with just enough room for a man to squeeze under to begin his day's work underground. Iron bars now block the entrances, but occasionally the miners' stories still escape, out into the open air, for all who will listen.

Still life in tangerine and green.

Web imitation of inverted Mt Fuji.

Slightly less than 4.0 miles from the trailhead (2.0 miles past the footbridge), Belgian Loop Trail (#624) will come in on your left. Stay straight. After crossing Barren Fork, Taylor Ridge Road dead-ends on your right. Follow this gravel road just a few yards until you see on your left the Sheltowee Trace slide back into the woods.

For the next mile, the trail continues to follow Barren Fork downstream, before the Sheltowee crosses a small concrete ramp and intersects with the

Nature's swirl of color and texture.

other side of the Belgian Loop. Bear right to stay on the Sheltowee. Follow yet another gravel road (leading to the 4-H camp) up a small hill, before the trail once again slips left back into the woods.

Shortly after both Barren Fork and the Sheltowee join Indian Creek, there is a nice campsite on your left, overlooking the water. This is a great place to drop packs, set-up

Backpacking Kentucky

Not quite ADA-approved, but still amazingly level.

camp, and rest a bit. You can then day-hike the rest of the trail, allowing you to explore the rock formations without carrying a load on your back. From camp, you can either hike out to KY 700 or turn back around and take in the scenery, as you head back west to the US 27 trailhead.

Side Trip: From the KY 700 trailhead, you are only 15 minutes to Cumberland Falls State Resort Park, which has about 20 miles of trails. Cumberland Falls, home of the "Moonbow", is always quite impressive. The easy 1.5-mile hike to 44-foot tall Eagle Falls is well worth your time. You can learn more at the park's website tinyurl.com/CumbFalls.

Sheltowee Trace National Recreation Trail:
24. Mark Branch and Gobbler Arch

This overnighter includes a beautiful creek walk along the Sheltowee Trace.

Trail Length: 8.1 miles
Suggested Time: 2 days / 1 night
Maps: US Forest Service: tinyurl.com/Trace37
US Forest Service: tinyurl.com/GobblersArch
US Forest Service: tinyurl.com/MarkBranch
OutrageGIS.com: Sheltowee Trace Map—South

Overview: What? 8.1 miles? I bet you're thinking that you could do this as a day hike. And you could. But for most of you reading this book, it's a bit of a drive to the trailhead. Plus few opportunities exist to utilize local trails and create any kind of loop with the Sheltowee Trace. And this section of the Sheltowee is a beauty. The trail leads you to Mark Branch Falls and a simply gorgeous rockhouse, before the path winds its way along and through Mark Branch. The loop portion of the trail takes you down to Rock Creek and then up to Gobbler Arch, before returning back to the magical charm of Mark Branch.

Directions: From Whitley City (just south of Somerset, KY) follow US 27 south. Turn right (west) on KY 92 and drive for 6.5 miles. Immediately after crossing the Big South Fork River at Yamacraw, turn left on KY 1363. Drive 11.2 miles, following the signs for Bell Farm Horse Camp and Peters Mountain. At the turnoff for the camp, continue straight on FDR 139, heading towards Peters Mountain. Drive 4.4 miles. At the T-intersection of FDR 139, with FDR 6101 (on your left) and FDR 569 (on your right), bear slightly left and drive up into the trailhead parking area. (A note of mild caution: Many maps are way more confusing than the directions above. It's not that complicated.) The parking lot at Peters Mountain trailhead has vault toilets, but no water.

Staging: There is no camping at the trailhead. But you are deep in the Daniel Boone National Forest and you can camp just about anywhere, given the setback requirements outlined previously.

Route Description:
Sheltowee Trace—2.3 miles
Gobbler Arch Trail—3 miles
Mark Branch Trail—1.2 miles
Sheltowee Trace—1.6 miles

After parking, walk back across the road to find the trailhead for the Sheltowee Trace, directly across from the large, well-loved Peters Mountain sign. The first 0.25 miles of hiking is through a nice hardwood forest, but the terrain quickly steepens, as rhododendron hells and

121

Mark Branch & Gobbler Arch

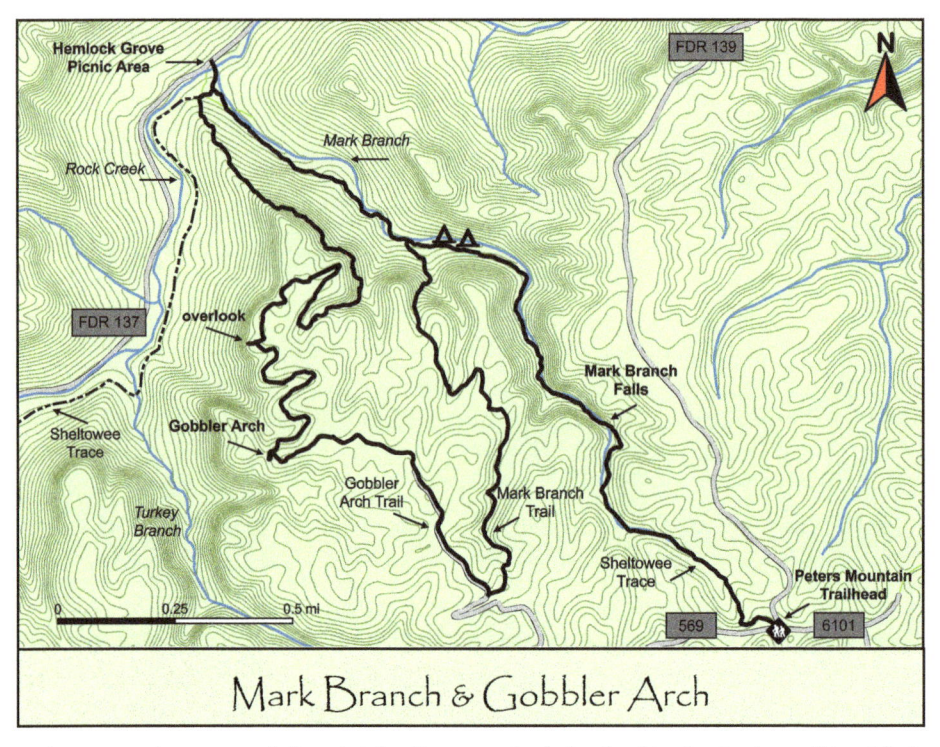

rock outcroppings appear left and right. Be sure to look for the faint beginnings of tiny Mark Branch—you will soon be awed by the power of its flow.

Speaking of water flow. As you read above, this section of the Sheltowee runs along and right through Mark Branch creek. While the wildflowers and falls are stunning here in spring, after a heavy rain this creek can get rocking. So choose the timing of your trip wisely and be prepared.

In another 0.5 miles, you'll soon hear falling water as the trail descends a steep set of rock steps into a magnificent bowl-shaped rockhouse. From the upper lip of the rock face, Mark Branch Falls plunges 80 feet into a pool of water, comfortably cushioned with light-colored sand. Even in the dead of summer, spring-fed Mark Branch creek gives quite a show. Iron oxide has leached from many of the rock walls, creating red, orange, and rust-colored hues, complemented by the green of the majestic hemlocks reaching up for the sunlight. Can you tell I like this place? Take your time here. It's a short hike and you'll want to savor the moment.

As you slowly make your way downstream, according to the US Forest Service, the Sheltowee Trace crosses Mark Branch 17 times. That seems a little bit of an exaggeration, but given you are hiking in the creek part of the time, it's difficult to count. At times you might feel like you are in a small slot canyon, with house-sized boulders left and right of the creek bed, while quartz pebbles sparkle underfoot. The sun rarely reaches many parts of the trail, making it difficult for the rhododendron to set bloom, but the lush, green moss is in heaven. Lucky for us, few people hike along Mark Branch.

In only 1.5 miles from the trailhead, the best camping spots of the hike can be found on your right, between the trail and the creek. Look sharp here because at mile 1.6, Mark Branch Trail comes in on your left. The trail sign is long missing, but several pieces of

Mark Branch Falls in mid-summer.

red plastic tape dangle from a large rhododendron marking the turn-off. You can hike the loop either way—the entire loop is approximately 4.9 moderately-difficult miles. Options include stopping here, setting up camp, and then day hiking the loop. Or continuing to carry your pack. Either way, let's assume you hike the loop counterclockwise.

Continue along the Sheltowee Trace for another 1.7 miles, until you reach a small opening in the woods, punctuated with wild cane. If you want to ford Rock Creek (a State

Wild and Scenic River, known for its rainbow trout) and visit the Hemlock Grove Picnic Area, head about 1 o'clock to the other side of the opening and find the short trail to the river. The land surrounding Hemlock Grove was purchased in 1935 from the Stearns Coal and Lumber Company, which had mined and clear-cut much of the area. In 1998, the picnic area suffered significant tornado damage. The Forest Service was able to salvage many hundred-year old hemlock logs. The wood was used to build the picnic shelter, which is supported by massive 10x10 inch timbers. Unbelievably, little evidence of damage exists today of the havoc nature wreaked.

Back where the Sheltowee entered the field, a sign on your left directs you to Gobbler Arch Trail. Although the sign indicates the trail is 0.25 miles from here, it's actually less than 100 yards. So bear left (west) on the Sheltowee and take another left on Gobbler Arch. Almost immediately Gobbler Arch Trail steeply ascends, gaining almost 350 feet in 0.4 miles. Over the next 0.4 miles, the trail follows the base of 200-foot sandstone cliffs, before taking you atop the ridge. The ecosystem quickly transforms itself from rhododendron, magnolia, and fern to mountain laurel, maple, and sassafras. About 1.5 miles from where you started the Gobbler Arch Trail, there is a small overlook with a good view off to the west, overlooking the valley cut over time by Rock Creek. The view is particularly good in the autumn with a blaze of color, although the ridgetop is covered in mountain laurel blooms in early May.

In another 0.5 miles, the trail ducks under Gobbler Arch, which always seems to funnel a nice breeze, even on the hottest of days. The arch is not particularly tall—measuring only twelve feet interior height—but it's an interesting example of an arch formed by two eroding rock houses on opposing sides of a narrow ridge. Continue along the trail as it climbs above the arch and in a few minutes you'll see an old logging road come in on your left. Stay straight here and climb over the large downed tree. You should see another white diamond blaze shortly on your right, confirming you're still good.

Gobble Arch Trail then joins an old gravel road. Stay on this for less than 0.5 miles and just before the road bends to the right, you'll see an old dilapidated sign for Mark Branch Trail on your left. Despite the signs condition, the trail itself is in remarkably good shape. It's a little over a mile from the Mark Branch trailhead to where it joins the Sheltowee at Mark Branch creek. You should see the red pieces of tape on the rhododendron at the trail intersection mentioned previously.

Turn right (east) to trace your steps back on the Sheltowee. The camping spots are just on your left. Enjoy the walk back along the creek to the falls and the imposing rockhouse—they are just as beautiful as the first time you saw them.

Sign for Mark Branch Trail.

Side Trip: In Whitley City, there is a small bakery and restaurant tucked away at 18 S. Main Street. Kristina's Kitchen has an extensive selection of fresh-baked goodies, as well as many vegetarian and gluten-free options on their menu. Open Monday through Friday, 8:30 am to 5:30 pm (closes at 3:30 pm on Fridays). kristinaskitchen.org. (606) 376–3422.

Sheltowee Trace National Recreation Trail: 25. Thru-Hiking the Sheltowee

Stretching well over 300 miles, the Sheltowee is easily the longest trail in Kentucky.

Trail Length: 322.5 miles and growing
Suggested Time: 20 to 30 days; or much more / much less
Maps: The Sheltowee has been rerouted in several places over the years. Be sure you have up-to-date maps and other information.
US Forest Service: tinyurl.com/STMapInfo (or tinyurl.com/Sheltowee)
US Forest Service: tinyurl.com/STSectionMaps
OutrageGIS.com (or sheltoweetrace.com)—for print and GPS downloads

Overview: The Sheltowee Trace (ST) is considered Kentucky's version of the Appalachian Trail. You can hike the whole thing in one fell swoop, or divide it into sections. There are pros and cons of hiking the ST north to south or vice-versa. The southern end is a little warmer year-round, but typically only a few degrees.

Directions:
Northern Terminus—From I-64, just outside of Morehead, KY take exit 137. Travel north on KY 32 for 1.2 miles. Take a right on KY 377. Drive another 15 miles. Parking is available at the trailhead, which starts on the eastern side of the road.

Southern Terminus—From Whitley City, KY follow US 27 south, until you are just a few miles south of KY 297 and a few miles north of Robbins, TN. After crossing over the New River, turn right onto Mountain View Road. After you turn, drive 5.3 miles, following the signs to the Burnt Mill Bridge trailhead, on the western side of the bridge.

Route Description: Gosh. Where does one begin? If you want to hike the whole thing, the Sheltowee Trace Association (STA) is a good place to start. STA has done a great job of planning improvement projects, organizing work groups, rerouting the trail where needed, advocating for the Trace, and organizing thru-hikes. See www.sheltoweetrace.org/.

Each year the STA runs a "Hiker Challenge," which orchestrates thru-hikers into groups, enabling backpackers to hike the entire Trace over the course of a year. Two teams are developed, both of which hike one weekend a month (with the exception of December), beginning in January at the Southern terminus. Doing the math, that equates to about 30 miles of backpacking each weekend. Obvious advantages are the camaraderie of having fellow hikers join you out on the trail, sharing both shuttles and trail knowledge, while working toward a common goal. Estimated costs are about $40 a month.

OutrageGIS serves as the altruistic "commercial" partner of STA and they run the web site www.sheltoweetrace.com, which offers maps for sale, runs an on-line forum, and maintains a GPS mapping effort of the entire trail. Plus, if you simply Google "Sheltowee Trace" there are several blogs out there that may be of interest.

Backpacking Kentucky

Most people hike the Sheltowee Trace outside of the STA umbrella and most hike the trail in sections. In addition to entries #22, #23 and #24, sample sections of the Sheltowee Trace that have been combined with other trails and described elsewhere in this book include:

- Caney Loop *(at Cave Run Lake)*
- Chimney Top Creek *(an out-and-back in the kid's section)*
- Heart of the Gorge *(includes a small section of the Sheltowee)*
- Rockcastle Narrows East—Vanhook Falls *(utilizes other DBNF trails to make a loop)*
- War Fork and Resurgence Cave *(an out-and-back in the kid's section)*
- Yahoo Falls Loop *(utilizes other Big South Fork Trails to make a loop)*

Part 2: Backpacking with Children

Growing the Next Generation
of Happy Backpackers

Joys and challenges of backpacking with children

The advantages of kids being outdoors is well known—not only is being physically active good for the body, it's good for the soul. The same benefits we derive from hiking and backpacking, can also be derived by our children. And if we want to protect our environment for generations to come, we need to teach each and every new generation what the outdoors is all about. So get your kids outside early and get them outside often!

Backpacking with kids has some of the same challenges that many adults face. Kids get hot. Kids get cold. Kids get hungry. Kids get tired. But backpacking with kids also brings new challenges given their shorter attention spans, reduced stamina, and lower emotional intelligence. (*Sorry, but throwing that tantrum will not make the trail any shorter.*) So thinking about these challenges a little bit more and planning ahead will take you and your kids a lot further down the trail to backpacking nirvana.

Here are a few tips:

Start local. Really local.
Make your back yard (or a friend's back yard) your first tenting experience. Kids love this. They can help set up the tent. Chase fireflies in the evening. Eat snacks outside. Read at night with a headlamp and good book. And maybe cook breakfast over a camp stove.

Head to a campground.
It can be full-facility, with flushing toilets and electrical hook-ups, or even a walk-in site. Set up camp and then hike a short trail. Have kids carry something—a granola bar in his or her back pocket or a water bottle in their school pack. Head back to camp and go through all the motions of "camping out."

Engage kids in the planning process.
Have a few short trails in mind—usually 0.5 to 3 miles is a good starting point, depending on the age of your child. Pull out some maps and talk it over with your family. Explain to the kids how much of a drive it is to each trail, how long the trail it, what you might see, and so forth. Let the kids decide which trail to take. Just be sure to adjust your expectations down in terms of mileage, particularly for new backpackers.

Brainstorm with the kids on what gear to take. Let them make the first stab at compiling the list and then flesh it out as needed. When it comes time to pack, let them work to assemble the gear all in one room. Try not to pack for them!

How much weight should my child carry?
Every kid should have a backpack and carry at least one personal item. Yes, every kid. Even if it's a furry panda bear daypack with a snack inside, the symbolism is strong. As the kid grows, add more weight and more responsibility for shared items such as a cooking pot or tent stakes.

Backpacking with Children

The general rule of thumb for backpack load weight is 20% of the child's body weight. So a 50-pound kid can carry 10 pounds. You can pick-up an inexpensive (less than $10) suitcase scale that hangs over a door frame to weigh your packs. If the trail is flat, you can add a little weight, but if you expect elevation changes, lighten their loads. If anything, error on the side of their packs being too light rather than heavy. Be sure to allow each kid to bring one or two small extra things, perhaps a toy figure or stuffed animal. Paperback books and cards are great tent-time activities.

100% organic hotdogs.

Eat healthy foods.
You know what healthy foods are. Don't slack off just because the kids are coming along. Again, engage kids in the planning process. But also bring a few small treats to enjoy on your adventure. Maybe a chocolate bar for snack. Sausage on a stick for dinner. Or even a few marshmallows for the campfire. But pull these special foods out as a surprise and not as an expectation. And avoid using food as a reward.

Also be sure that your kids are staying hydrated on the trail. Water is essential to regulating internal body temperatures and keeping energy levels up. It's a good idea for each kid to carry their own water bottle, if they can manage the weight.

Red eft (juvenile red-spotted newt).

Make the trail fun.
Most kids are not linear thinkers, let alone linear hikers and frequently the things off-trail are more interesting than those found on-trail. So stop and look at that millipede or fungus. Count the spots on the red eft and see if he really has four toes on his front feet and five on his back feet. Play games like I Spy. Or see how many different wildflowers you can find. Tell knock-knock jokes. Tell stories.

Share chores.
At camp, everyone should have a chore. Even toddlers can pick up sticks. Older kids can help cook. And everyone can wash dishes.

Bring friends.
Choose carefully here, or you might have someone else's little terror. But consider inviting another family or a school buddy. Kids can encourage each other in so many healthy ways. Then take lots of pictures to reinforce that the trip was actually lots of fun.

Backpacking Kentucky

Smile in the face of adversity.
If you're bummed because it's raining, your kids will be too. If you think the sound of coyotes howling at night is really cool, so will they. Your kids look up to you for leadership, so be sure to watch what you say and do, and how you project yourself. Body language can say it all.

Teachable Moments.
Be prepared to share your knowledge on the trail without being a know-it-all. Talk to your kids about Leave No Trace Principles or about the importance of not shortcutting switchbacks. Bring a star chart, animal tracking book, or compass and navigation guide. Practice tying knots and sharing what they're useful for. Then just sit around and giggle.

Finally, if your first backpacking trip is not a smashing success, that's OK. Talk it over with your child and find out what could be done to make it better. And always be sure to ask your kids what they liked about the trip so you can repeat those choices next time.

The edible "chicken of the woods" mushroom.

The trails described below are a small sample of kid-friendly backpacking hikes to get you thinking about possibilities. Just remember to start small and soon your kids will be outpacing you!

All kids love goofy pictures. (J. Flores)

Big South Fork National River & Recreation Area:
A. Blue Heron Loop Trail

Outdoor park attractions without the crowds, glitter or price.

Trail Length: 6.2 miles
Suggested Time: 2 days / 1 night
Maps: National Geographic Trails Illustrated: Big South Fork
National Park Service trail brochure: tinyurl.com/glofdph

Overview: This is a great trail for kids that have had some backpacking experience or even for adults who want an easy day on the trail. The Blue Heron outdoor museum, run by the National Park Service, celebrates and remembers those individuals who gave their lives for the coal industry. Blue Heron, aka Mine 18, was a coal mining community on the Big South Fork of the Cumberland River that operated from 1937 to 1962. Once the mine closed, most of the buildings were torn down. However, in the 1980s the National Park Service recreated the community by building ghost structures of some of the original buildings, collecting tons of old photos, and recording hours of interesting oral histories. There is no charge to tour the mining camp. More information about Blue Heron can be found at tinyurl.com/BHMCinfo.

The trail starts ridgetop, including visits to Devil's Jump and the Blue Heron overlooks, before dropping down between Cracks-in-the Rocks. Beach front or wooded camping is available at the river. For the second day, the trail continues along the river, before climbing back to the ridge.

Directions: From Whitley City, KY follow US 27 south. Turn right (west) on KY 92 and drive for 1.3 miles. Turn left (south) on KY 1651. Drive for 0.5 miles. Turn right (west) on KY 741 and follow for 0.7 miles. Take another right on KY 742 until you reach the Big South Fork National River and Recreation Area. Just after you pass the turn off for the Blue Heron Campground, turn left on Gorge Overlook Road, which leads to the Blue Heron and Devil's Jump overlooks. Drive 0.4 miles to the first parking lot, which will be on your left. You can start at the parking areas for either overlook.

Regulations: See page 12. Overnight camping in the Big South Fork requires a $5 permit, for parties up to six people. You can purchase the permit at the park, from local vendors or on-line. The outdoor museum is open April through October, but the trails are open year-round. Camping regulations are quite generous—sites must be 25 feet from any trail or other features such as a cave, rockshelter or historic structure. Remember to secure your food and trash from predators. Pets are permitted, but must be kept on leash not to exceed 6-foot in length.

Staging: If you want to lengthen this into an overnighter, you can easily stay at the Blue Heron Campground before or after your backpacking adventure.

Backpacking Kentucky

Blue Heron Loop Trail

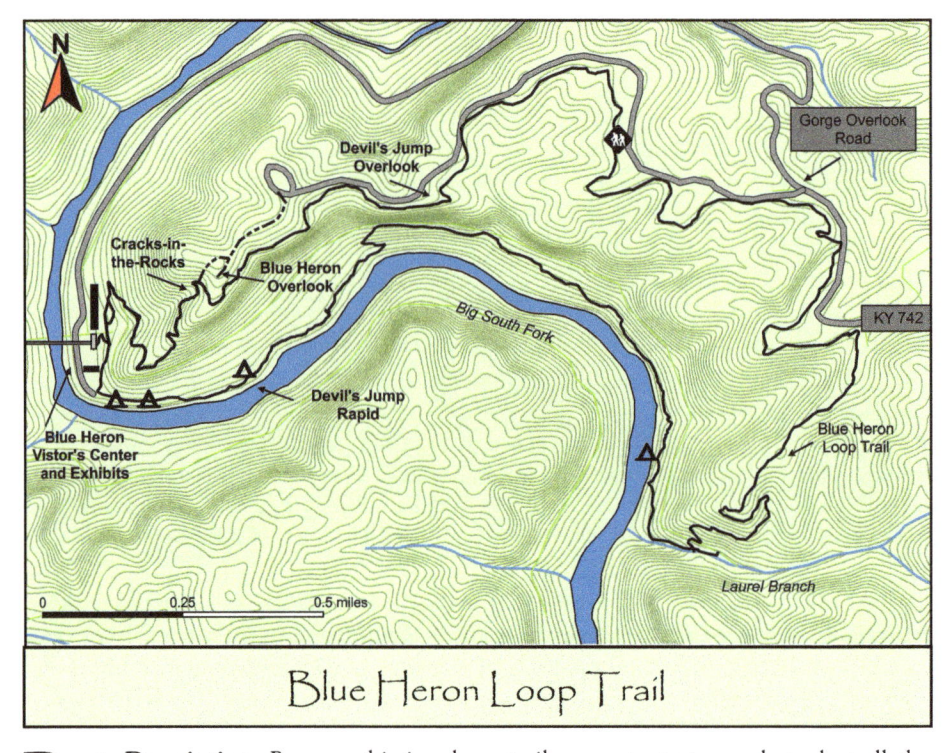

Route Description: Because this is a loop trail you can start anywhere, but all the camping is along the river. So it's best to start at the top and divide the trail into half. Don't underestimate your kids. Many youngsters can hike 3 miles without any problems. Just keep their packs light and avoid temperature extremes. Summers in southern Kentucky can be hot and sticky, and riverside camping can be quite humid. But with swimming and wading at your disposal, options abound. Just be prepared.

View from Devil's Jump Overlook.

Starting from the trailhead described above, take the Blue Heron Trail counterclockwise. Turn right and begin by heading north on the trail. For the first few minutes of hiking, there's not much to see as the trail parallels the road. But the kids will be excited to be here and in no time you'll be at Devil's Jump Overlook, named for the rapid seen far below and the nemesis of many a paddler. The overlook will give your kids a good sense of how much they will accomplish as they make their way down to the river and back up again, and will set the stage for your hike.

Backpacking with Children

Back on the Blue Heron loop, stay on the trail until you see the 0.2-mile spur to the Blue Heron Overlook. Bear right on the spur to make a small climb back to the top of the ridge. Again, enjoy the views of the Big South Fork (BSF) and the Cumberland River valley. The BSF is protected as a Wild and Scenic River, so please treat it with the respect it deserves.

Shortly after you begin your descent from the ridge, the trail climbs down a steep set of wooden stairs. At the bottom of the steps, a small spur trail takes off to your right. Definitely take the time to explore this area as it leads to a huge rockhouse and several walls which rock climbers frequent. Evidence of bolts on the rock is clearly visible.

The main trail then takes you to a popular place known as Cracks-in-the-Rocks. If you've not been here before, it is a really cool place that your kids will absolutely love. There are lots of nooks and crannies to explore and pictures to take. Again, take your time because you're only 0.5 miles to the Blue Heron Mining Community. Once down at Blue Heron, you can either explore the outdoor museum now, or head on over to the river and find a campsite first. The museum has lots to look at, so you may enjoy dropping your packs and then walking around the mining camp. Be sure to put walking across the tipple bridge on your to-do list.

As for camping, follow the Blue Heron Loop Trail past the boat launching area and head upstream along the river. On your right are several beach-front campsites with fire rings—yes, waterfront property for only 5 bucks a night. Or you can walk about 0.5 miles to Devil's Jump rapid. There is a wooded campsite on the opposite side of the trail, behind a large boulder, that stays nice and shady. This section of the trail is the best for spring wildflowers including trillium, Solomon's seal, crested iris, and wild geranium.

Devil's Jump Rapid at low water.

Backpacking Kentucky

The next morning, pack up your gear and continue making your way upstream along the river. After climbing a set of wooden stairs, the trail joins a horse trail, that is in very good to excellent condition. Bear right here and admire the striated rock that forms a wall on your left, solid evidence of the cutting capacity of the river over time. Just past a year-round spring, the trail crosses a small creek naturally tainted with iron oxide. After a little more walking, you'll come to a pine-needled camping site on a small bluff overlooking the river. This site appears to violate the 25-foot setback rule, but it's a popular location.

When the trail begins to bear east, you'll be following Laurel Branch, a really sweet little stream. After a steep ascent, the Blue Heron Loop Trail bears left up the steps. But stay straight on the trail just a few more minutes to get to the stream crossing and another maze of horseback riding trails. This spot stays cool and shady year round and makes a great lunch stop.

After returning to the main trail, climb the wooden steps and begin your ascent to the ridge by following a series of switchbacks. This is a good time to talk to your kids about the value of switchbacks and the erosion caused by those taking shortcuts. There's a nice rockhouse on your left that would cause Kobe Bryant to duck. Once you get close to the road, the trail levels off. Fortunately, road views are only intermittent and you're almost back to your vehicle.

Side Trip: If you or your kids are nuts about trains, try the Big South Fork Scenic Railway. The private company offers train excursions from Stearns, KY to the Blue Heron Mining Camp from April through October. For more information see www.bsfsry.com/.

Hiking across the tipple bridge.

Land Between the Lakes National Recreation Area: B. Canal Mini Loop

A more challenging hike for young kids, that easily can be made shorter or longer in length.

Trail Length: 3.8 miles, balloon loop (with many other options available)
Suggested Time: 2 days / 1 night
Map: US Forest Service: tinyurl.com/Canal Loop

Overview: Land Between the Lakes (LBL) has some mega kid-attractors. Water sports. Mountain biking. The Golden Pond Planetarium. The Homeplace 1850s Farm. The Woodlands Nature Station. Elk. Bison. So why not add backpacking to the mix? There are tons of options from easy out-and-backs to longer loops. Throw waterside campsites into the mix and you have a winner.

Directions: LBL is located just south of Grand Rivers, KY. To reach the trailhead, take exit 31 from I-24. Head south on KY 453 for 6 miles. KY 453 is also known as the Woodland Trace National Scenic Byway, or colloquially as "The Trace." The North Welcome Station serves as the official trailhead, although the trail can be accessed at many other points.

Regulations: You probably will want to read the previous section on the Land Between the Lakes area and the Canal Loop Trail in Part 1. A *backcountry* permit is required if you want to camp at the Nickell Branch Backcountry area. Permits can be purchased on-line or at the North Welcome Station daily from 9 am to 5 pm or after-hours at the Hillman Ferry Campground located just down the road. The permits are $7 for stays up to three days or $30 for an annual permit. Youth under the age of 18 are free. *Backpacking* permits are free if you want to camp outside of Nickell Branch and can be picked up at the self-serve kiosk just behind the North Welcome Station. Dogs are permitted on leash only.

Staging: The full-service Hillman Ferry Campground is 1.4 miles south of the North Welcome Station, just off KY 453. For more information see tinyurl.com/HillmanFerry. Other campgrounds are available in the park.

Route Description: If your kidlet is not too keen on backpacking or is totally new to the joys of sleeping outdoors, try an easy hike from the North Welcome Station to the Nickell Branch Backcountry Area. Head north on the Canal Loop Trail, which leads from the other side of KY 453. Yes, it's 2.6 miles one-way. But the trail is level to gently rolling and might remind you of an old wooden roller coaster where all riders must be 36 inches or less.

Nickell Branch has many amenities including picnic tables, fire rings, chemical toilets, and enough space to host a Rainbow Tribe gathering. But be forewarned—Nickell Branch can get quite rowdy, particularly on summer weekends. So if you're looking for more peace and quiet, and want to avoid the other tent and RV campers, there are several other camp spots before you get to Nickell Branch.

Backpacking Kentucky

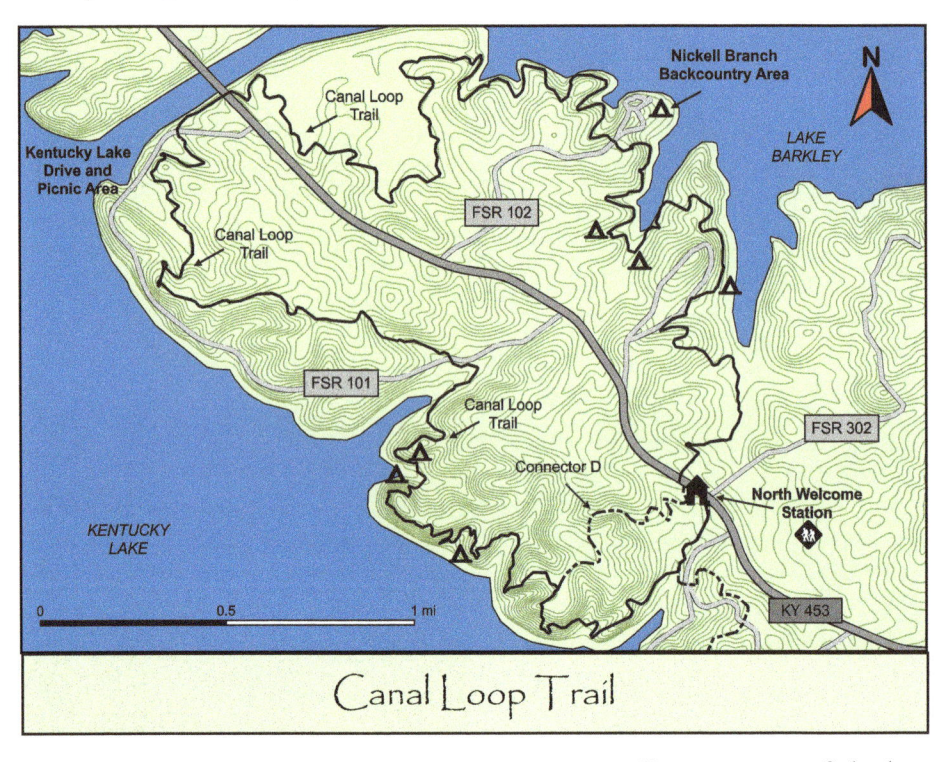

Canal Loop Trail

Shh...You might see a moose on the trail.

However, some of the best camping is on the other side of the Canal Loop Trail. If you like beautiful sunsets, rocky beaches, and quiet campsites, try the southwestern side of the loop. Again, you can do either an out-and-back or utilize the D connector trail to make a great loop hike. Or if you look at the on-line map, there are several other connector trails that could also be used to create loop hikes.

To take the more scenic route, head south from the North Welcome Station on the Canal Loop Trail. Be sure not to follow the paved trail, which leads to Hillman Ferry Campground. Right before you cross a small wood bridge, bear right to stay on the Canal Loop Trail, rather than bearing left for the North South Trail. Soon you'll get glimpses of Kentucky Lake, shimmering beyond the trees.

136

Backpacking with Children

Campsite overlooking Kentucky Lake.

One mile from the North Welcome Station, connector trail D comes in on your right. Stay left to get to the better camping spots. The shore is rocky here, as the stones are better for kerplunking rather than for skipping. Go wading or take a dip, before building a nice campfire along the shore. Slip those s'mores ingredients out of your pack and be prepared to make some good memories.

Side Trips: You could spend all week at Land Between the Lakes and still not see everything. The Woodlands Nature Center has lots of great kid-friendly activities including eagle tours, a hummingbird festival, and Howl-o-ween. They even have a dog kennel for Fido while you're touring. Cost is $5 for ages 13 and up; $3 ages 5-12; and free for ages 4 and under.

The Elk & Bison Prairie allows these magnificent mammals to roam across 700 acres of a native grassland habitat, similar to what was found here hundreds of years ago. Cost is $5 per vehicle.

The Golden Pond Visitor Center has many free exhibits exploring the historical and natural worlds of LBL. The Planetarium and Observatory are also located here, with fees varying by program.

Finally, the Homeplace 1850s Working Farm and Living History Museum features interpreters reenacting life on the farm, including quilting, looming, forging, rail splitting, cooking, and daily chores. Many rare breeds of farm animals are also housed here. Cost is $5 for ages 13 and up; $3 ages 5-12; and free for ages 4 and under.

For more information on all of these places, see www.landbetweenthelakes.us.

Laurel River Lake:
C. White Oak Boat-In Campground
D. Grove Boat-In Campground

Lakeside glamping for young backpackers—or anyone who's looking for a few creature comforts of home while out on the trail.

Trail Length: White Oak 2 to 3 miles; Grove 1.5 miles. (All distances round-trip.)
Suggested Time: 2 days / 1 night (or more)
Maps: USFS: tinyurl.com/White-OakCampground; tinyurl.com/GroveCampground

Overview: Laurel River Lake, created by the damming of Laurel River, is one of the largest lakes in Kentucky. The lake measures approximately 19 miles long and has over 200 miles of shoreline, with multiple coves and fingers. Average lake depth is 66-feet and fishing is excellent.

The lake has two walk-in/boat-in campgrounds, each accessible by relatively easy hikes. This really isn't pure backpacking per se, but it's a great way to introduce your kids to carrying their own gear, putting up a tent, cooking outdoors, and gazing at the stars. Each campsite has a picnic table, tent pad, fire ring, and lantern pole. Water and vault toilets are centrally located. Neither campground has an official beach, but swimming opportunities are plentiful.

The White Oak Boat-In Campground has 51 wooded, lakeshore sites that get busy on nice weekends during the summer, but never really fill-up. A quiet gravel road leads to the campground.

The Grove Boat-In Campground is close to Grove Marina and has a total of 37 sites. About one-half of the Grove sites are lakeshore, but many are not wooded. The campground is reached by the Duff Branch Trail.

Campsite at White Oak Boat-in Campground.

Backpacking with Children

Directions:

To the White Oak Boat-in Campground: From I-75, take the London exit #38. Travel west on KY 192 for 10.9 miles. Turn left (south) on Marsh Branch Road (signed for the boat ramp). Drive another 1.5 miles. Turn left and park in the small lot.

To the Grove Boat-in Campground: From I-75, take exit #25 and stay on US 25 west for 5 miles. Turn right on KY 1193. Drive 2 miles. Turn right on Grove Road (FSR 558). Drive 3 miles to the Grove Drive-In Campground. Register at the campground entrance gate. Park at the far end of the campground, Loop C, in the small lot reserved for walk-in campers. The trailhead to the Duff Branch Trail is off this parking lot.

Regulations: Both campgrounds are open mid-March through mid-October. Self-serve pay stations are located at each campground. Fees are $16 per site (single) or $26 per site (double). Cash is always good. Checks can be made out to "American Land & Leisure", the concessionaire who operates the campgrounds for the Forest Service. Dogs should be on leash.

Hiking the road to the White Oak Boat-in Campground.

Backpacking Kentucky

White Oak Boat-In Campground

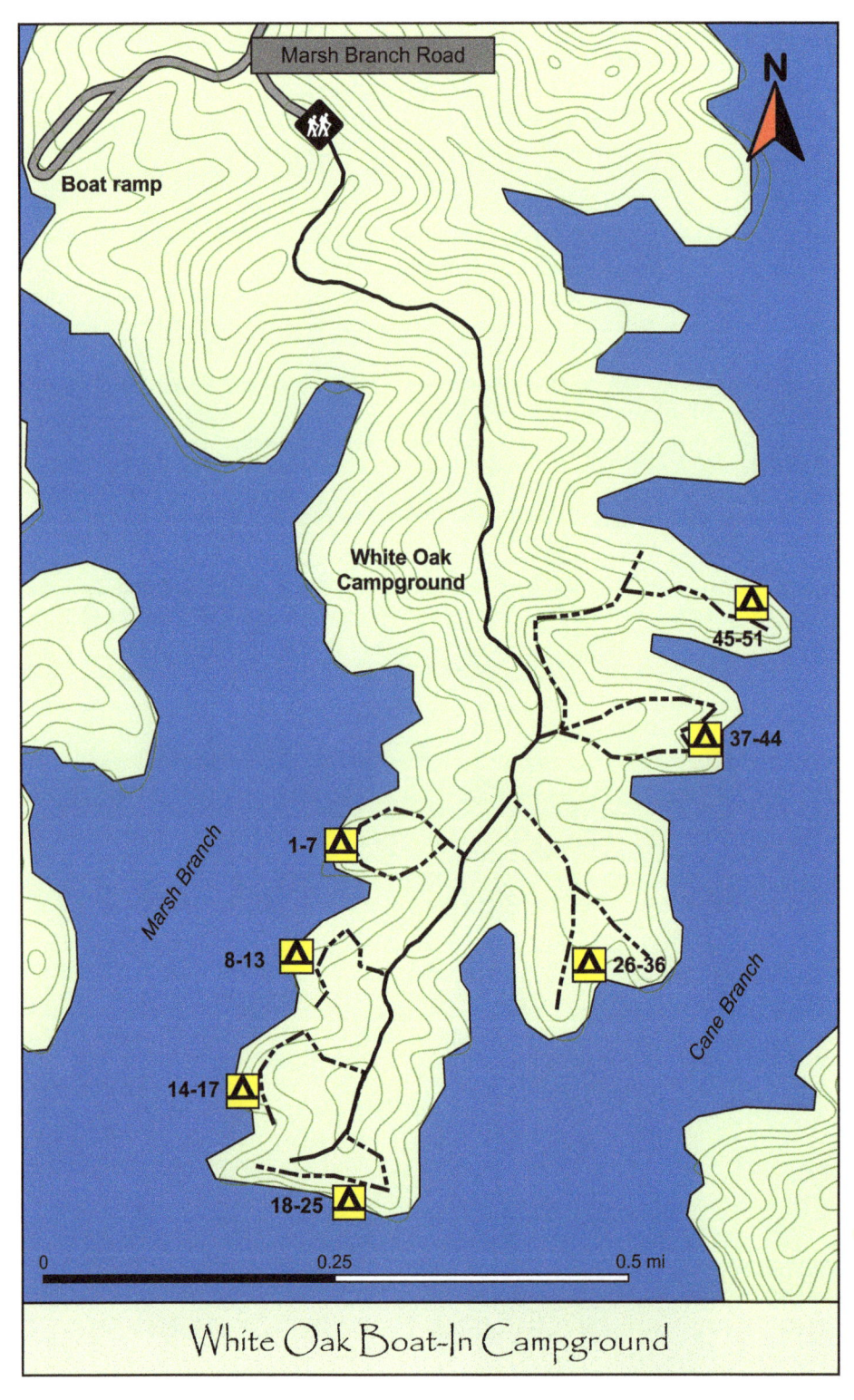

140

Backpacking with Children

Route Descriptions:

White Oak Campground: To reach the White Oak Boat-In Campground on foot, you have two basic choices. The first is to follow the 3-mile Cold Rock School Trail, which is overgrown, rarely scenic, and full of poison ivy. Your second choice is to simply follow the gravel service road (FSR 772) for about a mile until you reach the campground. The road is level to rolling, passes through a beautiful deciduous forest (complemented with ferns, hemlocks, pines, and hollies), and allows you and your junior partner to walk side-by-side, discussing the merits of Nutella versus cookie dough ice cream.

In about 0.85 miles of walking the road, you will reach the first of several different gravel paths leading to multiple camping options. Each cluster of tent sites has vault toilets, garbage cans, and potable water. In general, all of the sites are well spaced from one another, have well-drained tent pads, and are fairly close to the water's edge. While there are few sandy beaches, the number of skipping stones available will keep you busy for hours. Early fall is a great time to be here, with fewer bugs, the water is still plenty warm for swimming, and that campfire at night feels great.

Grove Boat-in Campground: After driving through the Grove Campground and parking in the lot at the end of Loop C, find the trailhead to Duff Branch. Be forewarned, the parking lot serves both the walk-in and the boat-in campsites! The walk-in sites are accessed at the far (northeast) end of the parking lot. You should take Duff Branch Trail, which leads, from the southwest edge of the lot.

The trail is a 0.7-mile, gravel service road that splits at the Y. The left-hand spur leads to the smaller peninsula with six campsites, and the right-hand spur leads to the larger peninsula with 31 sites. Most of these sites are ridgetop, rendering water access a little more difficult, and many sites are not shaded. Since Grove is also close to the marina, there's a lot more boat traffic on this side of the lake. These caveats make White Oak Campground a better experience for many campers.

The parasitic Indian pipes or ghost plant.

Another Option: Clay Lick Boat-in Campground at Cave Run Lake is accessible by an easy 0.5-mile trail. Amenities are considered "primitive." For more information, see tinyurl.com/Claylick.

Side Trip: From Laurel River Lake, it's an easy drive to Scuttle Hole Trail, a 0.75-mile trail to three overlooks of the Rockcastle River and the way-cool Scuttle Hole. From KY 1193, turn west on KY 3497. Drive about 5 miles until you see the trailhead sign on your right. There is another trailhead further down KY 3497, located within the Rockcastle Campground, but it is not well maintained. tinyurl.com/ScuttleHole

Mammoth Cave National Park:
E. Homestead
F. First Creek Lake
G. Three Springs

Not all of the fun at Mammoth Cave Park is underground.

Trail Length: Homestead 4.4 miles; First Creek Lake 2.2 miles; Three Springs 1.6 miles (all distances round-trip)
Suggested Time: 2 days / 1 night
Maps: Mammoth Cave National Park: tinyurl.com/MCNPTrails
(Be wary—several trails have recently been rerouted and names changed. Many maps are no longer accurate. The new MCNP map noted above is correct.)

Overview: Lots of kids love exploring underground. Lots of kids don't. But any adventure that begins with a ferry ride brings out the kid in all of us. The hike to the Homestead backcountry site is pretty flat, making it an easy walk in the woods for most youngsters. The trail to First Creek Lake is downhill all the way—making it uphill on your return trip. And the hike to Three Springs has the best rock formations. All hikes are out-and-backs, so Homestead is 2.2 miles one-way; First Creek Lake is 1.1 miles one-way; and Three Springs is 0.8 miles one-way.

Directions: Traveling from north I-65, take exit 53. From the south, take exit 48. Follow KY 70 and KY 255 to the MCNP Visitor Center, about 15 minutes west of the interstate. This is a good time to talk to your kids about the symbolism of rebel flags and what "rock shops" are all about.

Regulations: All backcountry camping must be in permitted sites. Although free, permits must be picked up in person from the Visitor Center and no reservations are accepted. Be flexible since permits are available only on a first-come, first-served basis. Each backcountry campsite is permitted for one party, up to eight people, and two tents. Dogs are permitted on leash. No food storage requirements are in place, although hanging poles are available.

Staging: Only one full-service campground is located in the park, Mammoth Cave Campground. Maple Springs Campground only has seven sites: three are group sites and four are equestrian sites. The Houchin Ferry Campground is more "primitive," making it the preferred option for some. All campgrounds accept reservations. MCNP also cabins for rent.

Route Descriptions: A larger version of the accompanying map is on page 65. As you can see, there are lots of options with this spaghetti-junction of a trail system. So feel free to create your own backpacking trip to meet the needs of both you and your kids.

Mammoth Cave Trails

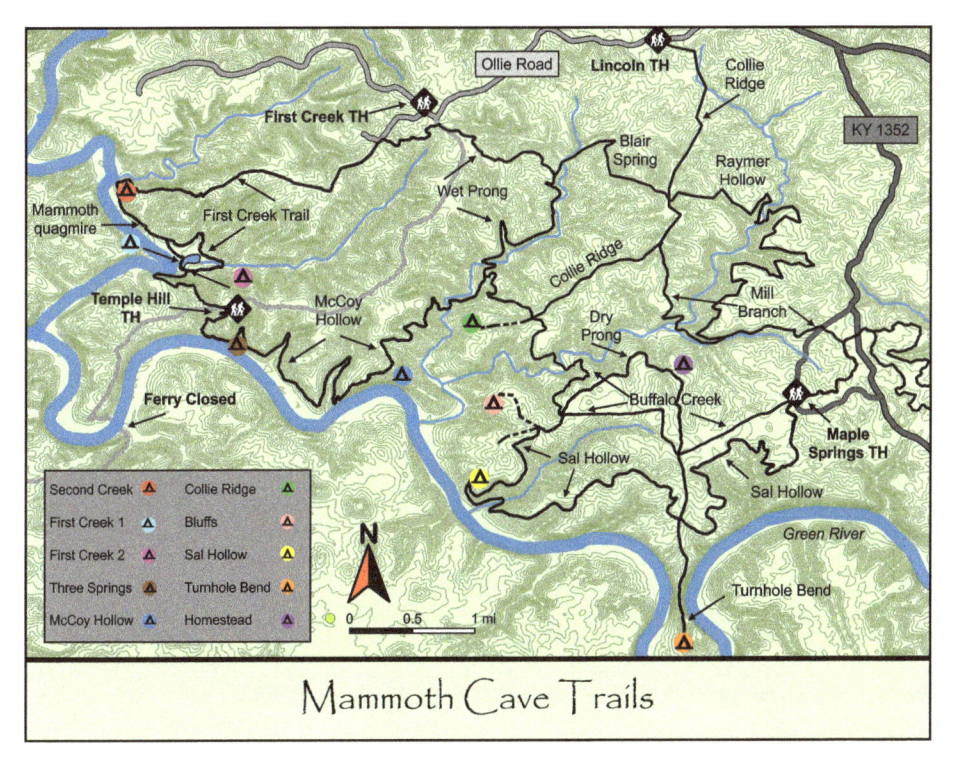

Homestead: After picking up your permit, head to the (free) Green River Ferry. It only holds two vehicles, but wait times are usually quite reasonable. From the ferry, follow the Green River Ferry Road north for about 2 miles. Turn left on Maple Springs Loop Road. Trailhead parking is available here.

From the trailhead, follow the Buffalo Creek Trail, an old road in relatively good condition, for 1.1 miles. At the trail junction, head north (take a right) on the Turnhole Bend Trail. This trail can be muddy in spots, but most of the year it's quite good. Walk 0.8 miles to the turn-off for the Homestead backcountry site. Follow this spur north for 0.3 miles.

Surprisingly, at the Homestead site there aren't any visible remains of any homestead. But the site is quite large, has one tent pad, a large fire pit, and a hanging pole. The area is mostly flat with several other well-drained tent sites. At the far end of the campsite, a very steep trail leads down to a creek and tumbling water. It's a fun place to explore, but quite a scramble to get back up!

First Creek Lake: Again, pick up your permit and cross the Green River via the ferry. Follow Green River Ferry Road (aka Maple Springs Ranger Station Road aka KY 1352) for 6 miles. Turn left on KY 1827. Drive 0.8 miles. Turn left on Ollie Road. Drive about 2.5 miles. Just past Mammoth Cave Horse Camp (which will be on your right), you will see a small gravel road on your left. Turn left on Houchins Ferry Road. Follow this gravel road about 4 miles until you reach the Temple Hill parking area. The trailhead is on the north side of the lot.

Follow the McCoy Hollow Trail towards First Creek for 1.1 miles. The trail has recently been renovated, and is in good shape and easy to navigate. Once you are close to the lake, a right-hand turn at the junction will take you east to First Creek Campsite 2 (it's marked "2" on the park map, but "B" on the sign). This campsite is very, very wet in the spring. But it is closest to the lake.

A left-hand turn at the junction takes you north to First Creek Campsite 1 (it's marked "1" on the park map, but "A" on the sign). Here the trail crosses a small bridge and you'll see the campsite on your left. While the view isn't quite as good here, the campsite is in much better shape—that is, much drier.

Both campsites have one tent pad, fire ring, and hanging pole. In your free time, you can hike the 1.0-mile loop that goes around the lake. This is a really pretty area, but can be quite wet in the spring.

Reflections on First Creek Lake.

Three Springs: Follow the directions to Temple Hill described above. The trailhead is on the south side of the lot. Follow the McCoy Hollow Trail for 0.8 miles. On trail-right you'll see the sign and small spur trail to the backcountry site. If you need to get water, just past the spur to the campsite the main trail crosses a small creek. The McCoy Hollow Trail is one of the best in the park—horses have done little damage to the trail and the rock formations are really great. (Note: River views are limited along this section of the trail after the trees have leafed out, despite what the map suggests.)

Side Trip: While at MCNP, your kids might be game for a cave tour. Several different kinds of tours are available, from historical to "domes and dripstones." The Trog Tour is open to kids ages 8-12; no parents allowed. The kids don coveralls, helmets, and headlamps before crawling around in the cave. All tours are ranger-led. You can check prices, availability, and make reservations on-line. Be careful to note the maximum number of people allowed on a particular tour. The size of some of these groups can really get large, particularly in the summer months. www.nps.gov/maca.

Backpacking with Children

Red River Gorge Geological Area:
H. Chimney Top Creek

A relatively flat trail that follows Chimney Top Creek, leading to campsites nestled under towering hemlocks, adjacent to large boulders and fun rock formations, and even the occasional pint-sized sandy beach.

Trail Length: 2 to 4.6 miles (round trip)
Suggested Time: 2 days / 1 night
Maps: OutrageGIS.com
Redrivergorge.com
US Forest Service: tinyurl.com/RRGorge

Overview: The Red River Gorge is one of the top backpacking destinations in Kentucky. Introduce your kids to what so many other hikers love about this area. The hike begins with a swinging bridge and ends with a crystal clear, cold water creek.

Directions: From exit #33 on the Mountain Parkway, turn north on KY 11 towards Slade, KY (away from Natural Bridge State Park). Drive back under the Parkway and turn left on KY 15. Drive 1.5 miles. Turn right on KY 77 towards Nada Tunnel and the Red River Gorge. Continue on KY 77 for another 5 miles, passing through Nada Tunnel. Do not enter the tunnel if you see oncoming headlights, as the 12-foot wide tunnel will not accommodate cars moving in opposite directions. The Dana Lumber Company built the old narrow gauge, railroad tunnel through 900-feet of solid limestone to extract lumber from the Gorge. Transpose Dana and voila… you get Nada (nay-duh).

Where KY 77 makes a sharp left turn, continue straight on KY 715 toward the Gladie Visitor Center. Drive 1.5 miles. Turn right on the gravel road (FSR 2126), signed for the Sheltowee Trace and Suspension Bridge. The short road descends to a good-sized parking area. If you reach the Gladie Visitor Center, you have gone 2 miles, too far. But Gladie is a great place to explore the history of the Gorge, so spending time here is a good thing.

Regulations: Don't forget your permit. See page 88.

Route Description: At the far end of the parking area is the trailhead. Be sure to hang your overnight permit on your rear-view mirror. Then follow the clearly-marked trail that heads upstream along the Red River for 0.4 miles. If it's a hot summer day, swimmers and canoeists will be taking advantage of the small gravel beach and deep pool at the base of the house-sized, jump-off rock. Another five to ten minutes of walking will bring you to the suspension bridge and the Sheltowee Trace Trail #100. The swinging bridge is tons of fun for kids of all ages, but may be a bit disconcerting at first. But once the kids get use to it, they'll want to cross several times.

After crossing the footbridge, bear hard right to stay on the Sheltowee Trace, which continues paralleling the river, but now heading downstream. The Sheltowee is blazed with white diamonds and a white turtle. About a mile from the TH (0.6 miles from the footbridge), the trail begins a gentle climb before reaching a small overlook of the floodplain at the confluence of the Red River and Chimney Top Creek. Down to your right you will see a small campsite in the floodplain below. The trail to the campsite is a bit of a scramble and in the summer the area gets rather weedy, harboring mosquitoes and chiggers. If you follow the trail a little more, the next campsite on your right (and on the opposite side of the creek) is a better choice, but you still get some road noise. Once you see the campsite, hike the Sheltowee just a few more minutes until you see a smaller trail leading down the hillside to the creek and access to the campsite.

But if your kiddos have the energy, and most of them do, keep on truckin' along the Sheltowee for another mile and better camping spots ahead. The trail climbs a nice set of switchbacks, creating an excellent time to explain why trails are not built straight up or down hillsides, and why hikers should not shortcut the switchbacks. About 1.9 miles from the TH, the trail crosses the creek, before crossing back again in another 50 yards or so. Again, use this as an opportunity to teach your kids about safe water crossings and be sure to look for the chubs, smallmouth bass, brown trout, and crawdads that call this creek home.

Suspension bridge over the Red River.

All of the campsites near the confluence of the Left and Right Forks of Chimney Top Creek, and near the intersection of the Sheltowee Trace and Rough Trails, are pretty sweet. The further you hike up into the drainage the larger the hemlocks, the greener the rhododendrons, and the colder the spring-fed water.

Other Options: Read the section on backpacking the Heart of the Gorge. There are several other kid-friendly options for youngsters including camping along Swift Camp Creek (excellent), Parched Corn Creek (a personal favorite, but it's only 0.6 miles one-way), and the ridgetop near Gray's Arch (be sure to watch the kids near the steep sections).

Dinner at Miguel's (pizza for the kids) or Rockhouse (maybe a cold beer for you) is always a perfect capstone to a great backpacking trip. For details, see Miguelspizza.com and Redriverrockhouse.com.

Every September the Gladie Visitor Center hosts the free Living Archeology Weekend, a totally cool event for kids. For more info, see livingarchaeologyweekend.org.

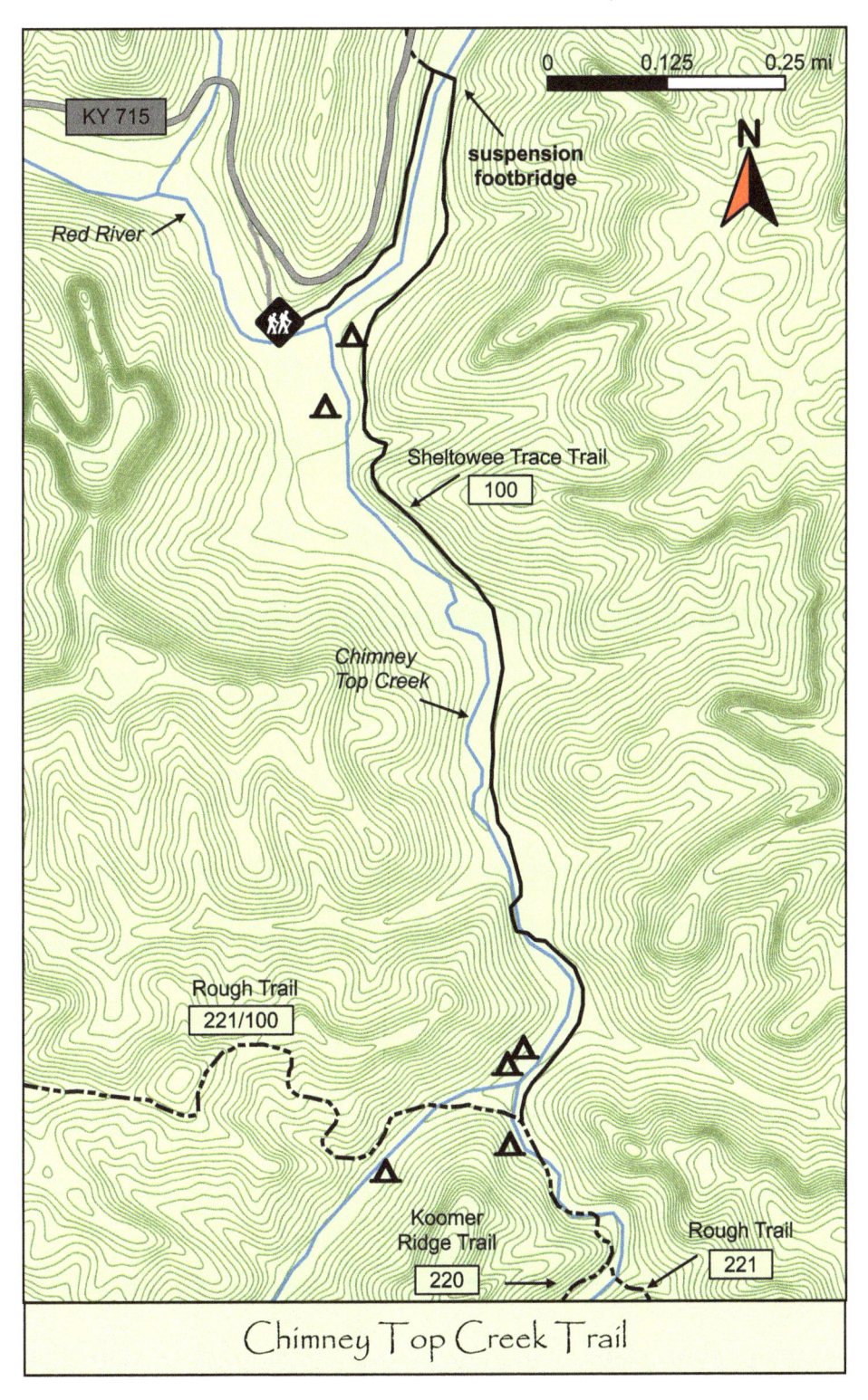

Backpacking with Children

Chimney Top Creek Trail

Sheltowee Trace National Recreation Trail:
I. War Fork Creek & Resurgence Cave

A great mix of backpacking and the joys of karst topography.

Trail Length: 3 to 5 miles, round-trip
Suggested Time: 2 days / 1 night
Maps: US Forest Service: tinyurl.com/TurkeyFoot

Overview: Spring-fed War Fork Creek stays cool all year long, making this hike a summer treat. And the waters flowing from Resurgence Cave adds bonus points to a great kid-friendly trail. You have two options here—a 2.5-mile hike (one-way), or cut it to 1.5 miles (one-way) if you need to take the easy way to find creek-side camping.

Directions: From McKee, KY, travel east on KY 89 for 3.1 miles. Make a right on Macedonia Road, drive another 0.5 miles, and then make a left on Turkey Foot Road. You should see a sign for the Turkey Foot National Forest Recreation Area. In about 1.0 mile, the paved road turns to gravel. Drive an additional 2.0 miles and turn left just prior to the bridge. This is Elsam Fork Road or FDR 345. Heed the flood prone area signs, as you must cross a small creek bed. Park in one of the gravel pull-offs. This is the upper trailhead. If you want the lower trailhead, drive another mile on FDR 345 and find a place to pull-off.

Regulations: No permits needed. For more information, see page 111.

Staging: Turkey Foot Campground, with 15 tent sites, is right at the trailhead and rarely full. Vault toilets. No potable water available. Open April through November.

Route Description: Now you see it. Now you don't. How much fun is that? Filled with spring rains, War Fork Creek chats noisily through the Daniel Boone National Forest. But as the water resides, long stretches of the creek stand silent and dry. Give your kids a lesson in karst topography and the chance to observe first-hand the effects of how water-soluble limestone creates an underground drainage system of sinkholes and caves. With the Sheltowee Trace trail paralleling both the forest service road and the creek, backpackers have an easy escape route if needed.

If you want to hike the whole thing, look for the trail heading off the road, across from the entrance to the campground. Hike up the small rise until you meet with the Sheltowee Trace. Turn right to hike the portion of trail that parallels the road. In about a mile, the Sheltowee crosses Elsam Fork Road (just around the bend in the road) and continues paralleling the road on the other side. This crossover point is the "lower" trailhead if you want to cut your distance. From where the trail crosses the road, it's less than 1.5 miles to camp.

A watchful eye might spot some of the morel mushrooms that inhabit this hillside in early spring or the beautiful large-flowered white trillium in late spring as you make your

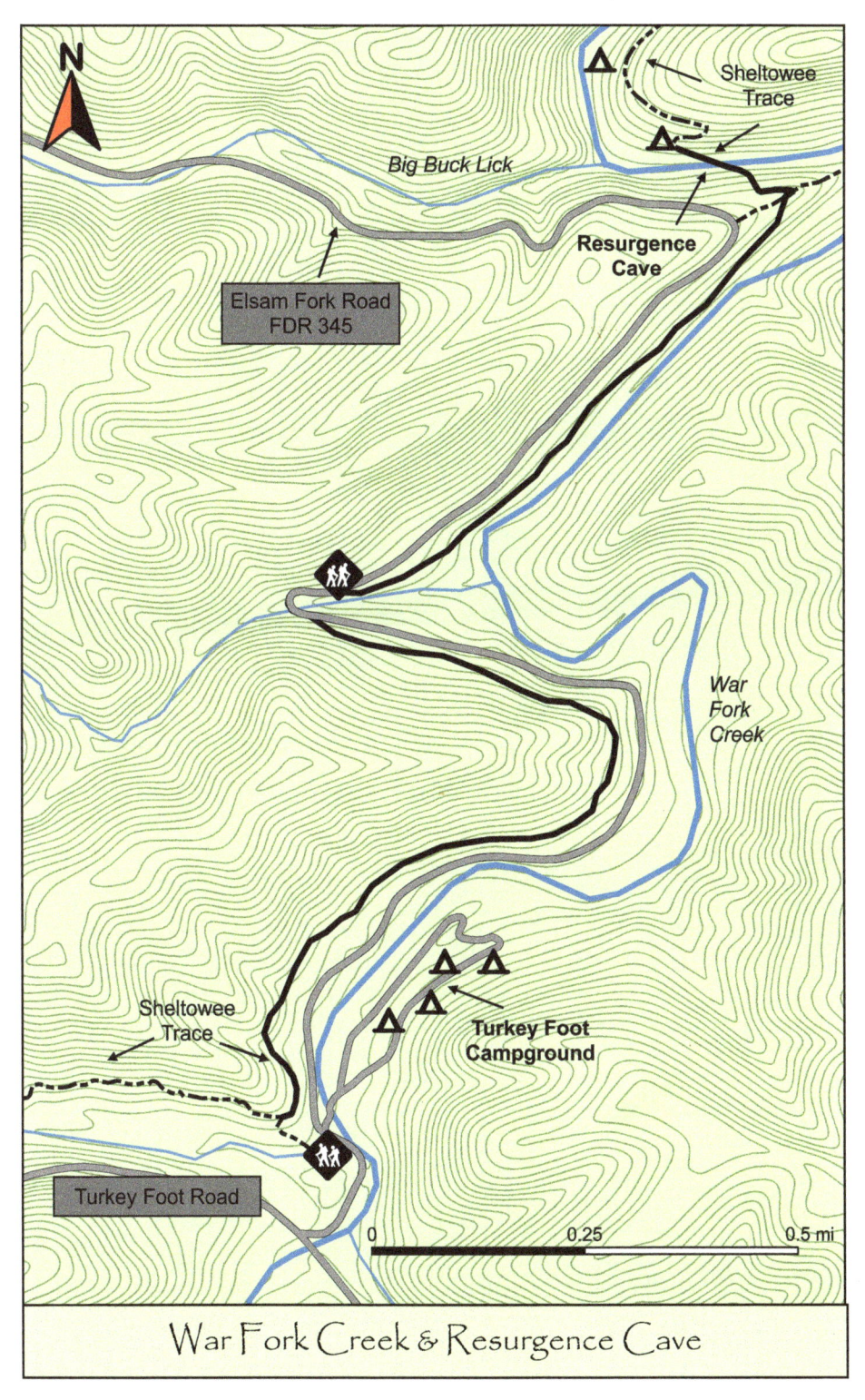

Backpacking with Children

War Fork Creek & Resurgence Cave

way closer to the creek. Once you reach War Fork, Resurgence Cave is located on creek-left, right at the stream crossing. Even in the dead of summer, 60-degree water flows from the cave, forming a small, but wonderful swimming hole just below.

Resurgence Cave at War Fork Creek.

You will have to cross the creek to reach the campsite. With the exception of early spring, this section of the creek should be nearly bone-dry. If not, make sure you have a stout walking stick and carefully make your way across. If by chance this campsite is occupied, there is another great site located further downstream, on creek right. Just follow the creek to find your spot under the canopy.

Side Trip: Beautiful Flat Lick Falls is only a 20-minute drive away. The paved trail to the falls overlook takes only five minutes, but there is another mile of dirt trail that leads along the creek and to the base of the falls. From Turkey Foot Campground, take a left on Elsam Fork Road and another left on Turkey Foot Road. Drive 1.8 miles. Turn right on KY 587 S and go 2.5 miles. At the stop sign, stay straight on KY 3445. Go another 2.3 miles. At the next stop sign, stay straight on KY 1071. Go another 2.4 miles. Cross US 421 onto Hays Road. Bear left on Lower Hays Road and follow the signs to Flat Lick Falls.

War Fork Creek is stocked with 2,500 rainbow trout annually, although it gets fished pretty hard by the locals. All fishing rules and regulations apply, but kids under 16 don't need a license or trout permit. Makes you want to be a kid again.

About the Author

After spending more than 20 years as a university researcher and professor, Valerie traded the ivory towers of academia for the great outdoors. Her background in natural resource economics and love of nature translated into a second career of writing outdoor guides, including "Hike the Bluegrass and Beyond," "Five Star Trails: Louisville and Southern Indiana," and "Fly Fishing Kentucky." An avid outdoorswoman, Valerie has swum in Africa's Lake Malawi, climbed China's Mount Tai, sailed the coast of southern France, biked Nova Scotia, and backpacked the überchallenging West Coast Trail of Vancouver Island. Her honeymoon was spent kayaking the Grand Canyon with her husband, Ben. The mother of four, Valerie lives in Lexington, Kentucky and hits the trail every chance she gets.

Photo by Emma Askren

Other books of interest

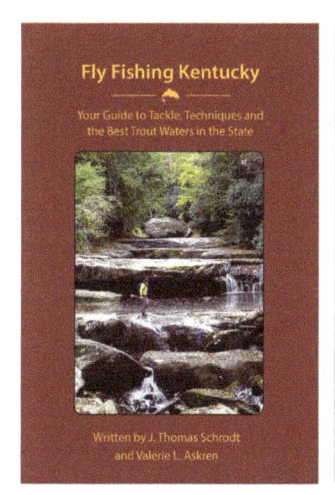

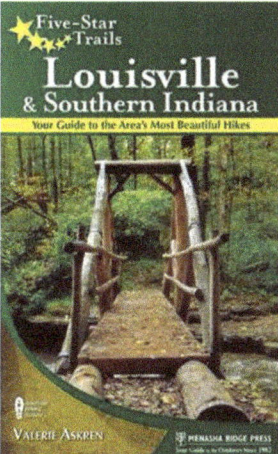

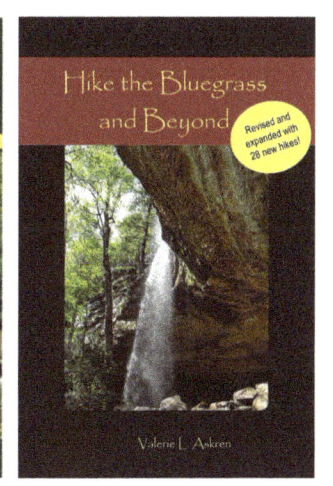

Tomorrow is a leg day.